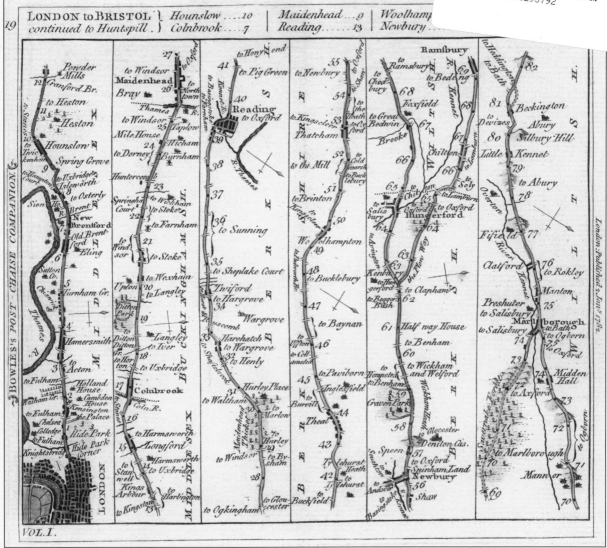

Morden's map of 1701

Bowles's Bristol/Bath Road map, 1782

STOKE POGES

A BUCKINGHAMSHIRE VILLAGE
through 1,000 years

View from the south of the old manor house with Thomas Penn and his family in the grounds. Engraved after a painting by H. Pugh, *c.*1765.

STOKE POGES

A BUCKINGHAMSHIRE VILLAGE
through 1,000 years

Lionel Rigby

Lionel Rigby

Phillimore

2000

Published by
PHILLIMORE & CO. LTD.,
Shopwyke Manor Barn, Chichester, West Sussex

ISBN 1 86077 131 9

Printed and bound in Great Britain by
BUTLER AND TANNER LTD.
London and Frome

Contents

List of Illustrations vii
Acknowledgements x
Subscribers xi

Introduction 1

One
The Origin of the Name 'Stoke Poges' 2

Two
The de Molyns Family 4

Three
The Hungerford and Hastings Families 7

Four
The Hastings Chapel and Almshouse 10

Five
Sir Edward Coke, the Great Lawyer 14

Six
The Owners of the Manor House from 1640 to 1760 16

Seven
Thomas Gray and Stoke Poges 18

Eight
Two Stoke Poges Sailors 22

Nine
The Penns 25

Ten
The Poor of Stoke Poges 30

Eleven
The House that Squib Built 32

Twelve
The Workhouse and Mrs. Parker Sedding 36

Thirteen
The Workhouse Rules 38

Fourteen
Mr Robarts the Surgeon 40

Fifteen
The Enclosure Controversy 42

Sixteen
Sidney Godolphin Osborne and the Poor Law Petitions 48

Seventeen
Stoke Park 1848-1908 54

Eighteen
Stoke Park—The Golf Club 56

Nineteen
Stoke Place and Stoke Green 60

Twenty
Sefton Park 66

Twenty-One
Stoke Court 72

Twenty-Two
The Dog and Pot—West End 80

Twenty-Three
John Thomas Bunby—A West End Character 86

Twenty-Four
The Early Years of the Parish Council 88

Twenty-Five
Two Stoke Poges Families and the Boer War 96

Twenty-Six
The Ancient Parish Changes to the Modern Parish 100

Twenty-Seven
The First World War—Those Who Died 104

Twenty-Eight
Fred Spring of Stoke Green 108

Twenty-Nine
Gray's Meadow is Saved 112

Thirty
Stoke Poges Gardens of Remembrance 114

Thirty-One
Stoke Park Conservation Area 118

Thirty-Two
The Schools in Stoke Poges 120

Thirty-Three
The Development of Bells Hill 124

Thirty-Four
The History of Stoke Poges Church 134

Elegy Written in a Country Churchyard 145
Notes 149
Index 151

List of Illustrations

Frontispiece: View from the south of the old manor house with Thomas Penn and his family in the grounds. Engraved after a painting by H. Pugh, *c*.1765.

1. Norman warrior 2
2. 'Stoke', possibly by John Speed 3
3. Domesday Book plaque 3
4. The de Molyns brasses 6
5. Robert Lord Hungerford's effigy 7
6. The churchyard of St Giles, *c*.1915 8
7. George Hastings (1488-1545) 8
8. Etching of the Manor House 9
9. The Hastings Almshouse, 1892 10
10. The Hastings Almshouse, 1999 11
11. Lord Hastings of Loughborough 12
12. Sir Edward Coke 14
13-14. Sir Edward Coke's monument 15
15. Wall painting of armorial bearings . . . 16
16. Part of John Rocque's map of 1761 . . 17
17. An invoice for goods 18
18. Plaque of Gray at Eton 18
19. Thomas Gray 19
20. Gray's pew 20
21. Gray's Elegy—an engraving 20
22. The mail coach preparing to leave
    the village hall 21
23. Ringers' commemorative card 21
24. Naval officer 22
25. The capture of the *L'Amazone* 23
26. Cartoon of John Penn 26
27. Bas-relief by John Deare 27
28. Replica of a bust of John Penn 27
29. St Giles' Church 28
30. Overseers' account book entry 30
31. Removal of Thomas Noris 31
32. Location of the Workhouse 32
33. 'Uplands', Rogers Lane 33
34. The Overseers' accounts for
    equipment for making beer 34
35. A record of payment 34
36. Joseph Perriman's receipt 36
37. Signatures of those attending a
    Vestry meeting, 1806 37
38. The workhouse rules 38
39. The surgeon's receipt, 1790 40
40. A surgeon's bill for medical attention . 41
41. Typical surgical instruments 41
42. John Penn 42
43. Lord Francis Godolphin Osborne's
    estate map, 1802 43
44. Manorial court record, 1809 44
45. Enclosure Act notice 45

46. Enclosure Award map, 1822 46
47. Part of Enclosure Award map, 1822 . . 47
48. The Easter Hunt 47
49. Sidney Godolphin Osborne 48
50. The former vicarage 49
51. The Eton Union Workhouse 52
52. Henry Labouchere, *c*.1850 55
53. 'The Ages of Love' by Bertwell
    Thorwaldsen 55
54. Stoke Park Mansion, 1892 55
55. Golf club entrance from Church Lane 56
56. The Mansion from the lake 57
57. The winter gardens 57
58. The dining room 57
59. Stoke Park Estate, 1909 58
60. The Great Western motor
    omnibus, 1907 58
61. The Mansion in the early
    20th century 58
62. Stoke Poges Golf Club—membership
    card, 1929 59
63. The Club House in 1916 59
64. The Manor House, 1918 59
65. Entrance gates off Stoke Road 60
66. Stoke Place, 1999 60
67. Map showing road diversion, *c*.1820 . . 61
68. The Orangery 62
69. Howard Henry Howard-Vyse 62
70. Sir Richard Howard-Vyse 62
71. Stoke Green 63
72. Stoke Green 64
73. Stoke Green Conservation Area 64
74. Sefton Park 66
75. Vesta Tilley, *c*.1906 67
76. 'Desert Rat' arm patch 67
77. 51st Highland Division 67
78. Symbol of the Afrika Corps 67
79. 1948 sale map of Sefton Park Estate . . 68
80. The main house 69
81. South Lodge 70
82. Cottage in kitchen garden 70
83. The Home Farm 71
84. East Lodge 71
85. Stoke Court, 1921 72
86. Auction particulars 73
87. The main residence 74
88. The chain of four lakes 74
89. The Stoke Court Estate sale map 75

90.   The main hall   76
91.   The library   76
92.   Stoke Court Estate sale map   77
93.   Plan for plots 28 to 33   77
94.   Winterclyde   78
95.   Stoke Court sale—home number 21 . .   78
96.   The adjoining cottage   78
97.   Two semi-detached houses   78
98.   Stoke Court Country Club   79
99.   Stoke Court fire damage, 1979   79
100. Certificate of membership of the
        Benevolent Brothers Friendly Society   80
101. The new *Dog and Pot*, 1900   81
102. The sub post office   82
103. James Langley   82
104. West End, now Rogers Lane   83
105. West End, 1897   83
106. Kiln Cottage   84
107. The site of the old brick kiln   84
108. Poor's Row front view   84
109. Poor's Row rear view   85
110. West End   86
111. Winterclyde   87
112. The Reverend Vernon Blake   88
113. Henry Allhusen   88
114. Duffield House, *c*.1903   89
115. Declaration of acceptance of office
        as parish councillor   90
116. Charles Simmons of Stoke Road   90
117. Stoke Road   91
118. Stoke House   92
119. The School Room at Stoke House . .   92
120. Jeremiah Albrow's message   93
121. The tradesmen of 1896   94
122. Advertisements, 1896   95
123. Charles Simmons' advertisement   95
124. Wives and families of the men
        serving in the Boer War   96
125. Mrs. Henry Allhusen   97
126. Wilfred Ward   98
127. Certificate presented to
        Louisa Ward, 1913   98
128. The scattered hamlets of Stoke Poges 100
129. Baylis House 100
130. The Great Western Railway 101
131. Horlick's factory 101
132. Slough's expansion 1894 to 1931 . . . 102
133. Agricultural advertisement, 1907 103
134. The First World War Memorial 104
135. Stained glass commemorating
        the Clifton brothers 105
136. FE 2b reconnaissance biplane 106
137. Royal Flying Corps badges 106
138. The grave of Second Lieutenant
        W.G.T. Clifton 106
139. The bellringers of 1913 108
140. The peal board 109

141. Invitation to servicemen, 1919 109
142. Returned servicemen 110
143. Terraced cottages in Stoke Green . . . 110
144. The 'lea' of the Elegy 112
145. Gray's monument 113
146. Ceremony in Gray's Meadow 113
147. Founder's stone, Memorial Gardens . 114
148. The Bishop of Buckingham, 1935 . . 114
149. Plan of Stoke Poges Gardens 114
150. Leading to the Colonnade 115
151. The old bell 115
152. Church Cottage, *c*.1920 116
153. Church Cottage, 1930 116
154. The Gurkha Memorial 116
155. Church Cottage, 1930 117
156. The Manor House 118
157. The Conservation Area 119
158. Historic views of Stoke Park 119
159. The old school house 120
160. The school in School Lane 120
161. Class of 1908 121
162. Maypole dancing, 1912 121
163. Class of 1919 121
164. Class of 1928 121
165-6. Stoke Poges First School
        playtime, 1976 122
167. The First School Centenary, 1976 . . 122
168. Centenary celebrations 123
169. Children playing Victorian games . . . 123
170. Bells Hill 1822, 1846 and 1959 124
171. The village hall 125
172. Looking north, Bells Hill 125
173. Letter received by Newell's 126
174. Miss Newell outside her shop 126
175. Bells Hill, 1965 127
176. Bells Hill, *c*.1920 127
177. Roy Neville outside his shop, 1927 . 128
178. Roy Neville's shop, 1930 128
179. Roy Neville outside his shop, 1969 . 128
180. The top of Bells Hill 129
181. Bells Hill, 1897 129
182. Squibb's general store on Bells Hill . 130
183. Walford's store, 1911 130
184. A team of postmen 131
185. Shop at the top of Bells Hill 131
186. Shops at the top of Bells Hill 132
187. The *Sefton Arms*, 1902 132
188. The *Sefton Arms*, 1928 132
189. The *Sefton Arms*, 1961 133
190. Bells Hill Shopping Precinct, 1969 . . 133
191. The Village Centre, 1997 133
192. Window in the north wall
        of the chancel 134
193. The oak timbered porch, *c*.1900 135
194. Interior of porch, 1999 136
195. Ground plan of the church 137
196. Stoke Poges Church, looking west . . 138

197. The Easter Sepulchre 138
198. The Hastings Chapel 139
199. The coat of arms of Lord Hastings . . 140
200. St Giles' Church, 1788 140
201. The Penn Pew 141

202. The Bicycle Window 142
203. The original Bicycle Window 142
204. The hatchment of Elizabeth Gayer . . 143
205. The hatchment of George Godolphin 143
206. St Giles' Church, *c.*1887 144

List of Colour Illustrations

    I Admiral Sir John Duckworth
   II The Allhusen coat of arms
  III Hatchment of Thomas Penn
   IV Hatchment of Granville Penn
    V Repton's map of Stoke Park
   VI Improved view of Mansion from Stoke Poges Lane approach
  VII Improved view of Mansion from Park Road approach
 VIII View of St Giles before Repton's improvements
   IX View of St Giles after Repton's improvements
    X Stoke Park Mansion, 1890
  XII Ditton Park, 1813
  XII Field Marshal Sir George Howard
 XIII Hatchment of Sir George Howard
  XIV Stoke Place
   XV Sefton Park Farm
  XVI Vesta Tilley—The Bold Militiaman
 XVII Sir Noel Mobbs
XVIII Stoke Poges Gardens of Remembrance
  XIX Aerial view of St Giles' Church

Acknowledgements

Whilst this book has been written in the main by Lionel Rigby, Trevor Harvey has researched and written chapter 27 on the First World War and Elizabeth Waghorn has written chapter 34 on the history of Stoke Poges Church. Ian Huntley has prepared the numerous illustrations and Frank Bowater has taken many of the photographs. Frank Bowater, Ian Huntley, Mike Milne-Smith and Lionel Rigby have edited and produced the final version of the book.

We would like to express our thanks to everyone who has helped in the production of this book and in particular the following:

John S. Adams, Bill Akerman, Naomi Arnold, Herbie Bacon, Toby Baillon, Mrs. V. Ballinger, Terry Brown, Tony Bunce, Peter Burgess, Tom Caldecourt, Dr. Robert Crocker, Reg Day, Dr. W.E. Duckworth, Reverend Mervyn Eden, Reverend Cyril Harris, L.H. Harris, E.C. Hartley, Clifford Hayward, R.E. Howard-Vyse, Dr. Judith Hunter, Henry Jolley, Hertford King, Eileen Loader, Tony Levings, Edna Mayer, Mona Morriston-Davies, Peter Neville, Janine Oliver, Barbara Rigby, Jane Rigby, Joyce Robinson, Douglas Sharp, Jean Simpson, Chris Stanley, Neil Stone, Judy Tipping, Angela Tuddenham, Eileen Wakefield, Don Wix and Stoke Poges Parish Council.

Thanks are also due to Julian Hunt and the Buckinghamshire Record Office; The Provost and Fellows of Eton College; Chris Furness, Paul Geehan, Roger Gill, David Green, Chris Marchant and Chris Popham of South Bucks District Council (successor to Eton Rural District Council); Cambridge University Press; Dean and Chapter of Salisbury Cathedral; Institut Royal du Patrimoine Artistique, Musée des Beaux-Arts, Brussels; The British Library; The Fitzwilliam Museum; National Maritime Museum; The Earl of Leicester and Coke Estates Ltd; Crane Davies Limited of the Manor House, Stoke Poges; Pauline Birger and the Bayer Group; Household Cavalry Museum; Greville Creative Group; Mander and Mitchenson Theatre Collection; The Pearce Rodgers Partnership; Slough Library; Slough Museum; Stoke Poges Parochial Church Council and the *Slough Observer*. We are also indebted to the late R.W. Cressy whose unpublished history of Stoke Poges, written in 1953, has been an invaluable source of information, and to the late Joan Philpot who was the librarian at Miles Laboratories, Stoke Court for many years.

We have made every effort to establish copyright where possible and obtain permission to reproduce, but if we have inadvertently omitted to do so for any particular photograph we offer our sincere apologies.

We are grateful for sponsorship from the following bodies and companies.
Bayer plc
Crane Davies Ltd.
Mobbs Memorial Trust
Pioneer GB Ltd.
South Bucks District Council
Stoke Park Club
Wexham Park Golf Club
an anonymous donor

List of Subscribers

Mrs. C.A. Adams
Felicity Jane Adams
Francis E. Adams
David and Mavis Admans
Dr. Penny Aeberhard
Dr. Peter Aeberhard
Nicholas Airey
Queenie M. Allen
William Allen
Stephen C. Anderson
Robert Ankers
Barbara Ansell
Jenny Arkell
Donald Arnold
Karen Arnold
Naomi Arnold
Mr. and Mrs. C. Aston
Dr. P.J. Atkins
Audrey
Roland and Susan Bailey
Alex and Rosemary Balfour
Mr. and Mrs. James C. Ball
Mrs. Jacqueline L. Barr
Charles and Karen Bates
Ros and Steve Batting
Michael Bayliss
Peter Beesley
Gerry and Vivien Begg
Roger T. Bell
Paul and Lesley Bensley and
   Family
Warner Benton
Mr. and Mrs. Philip Bergner
Stan Best
Mrs. Ann E. Biggs
Chris, Eileen, Jo and Sally Birch
Karen, Jenna and Tristan Blackie
Mrs. G. Bloor
Mr. N. Bloor
Mrs. Sybil Bowden
Mrs. Wendy J. Bowles
Mrs. Lynda Blunden (née
   Elderfield)
The Bracey Family
Matthew and Alison Brades
Barry Bradford
Peter and Eileen Bradley
Edward G. Brady
Michael and Janet Brent

S.M. Briant
Mrs. Norma Brice
Amanda Briggs
Reverend Gordon J. Briggs
Mrs. D. Brown
Frank and Margaret Brown
Hope Brown
Hugh Brown
Maureen Brown
Patricia Brown
Ruth Brown
Terry Brown
Alice Browne
Fergus Browne
Jack Browne
Mary and Derek Browne
Shirley Buckley
Carol Budd
George and Susan Bunby
A. Bunce
Peter Burgess
Councillor Patricia Burry
Patricia Ann Cahill
Kay, Gerald Calnan and Family
Catherine Carlow
Jean Carrod (née Evered)
Bryan Carter
Fiona Chandler
Edwina Chown
Jim Chown
Phoebe Claire
Emily Olivia Clark
Grace May Clark
Joyce Clarke
The Clay Family
David and Gay Claydon
Alexander le Clercq
'Nib' Cleveland
Michael Cole
Anne and Keith Collins
George A.G. Cook
Russell, Susan, Georgina and
   Luke Cook
Mrs. G. Strickland Cooper
M.J. Cooper
Clive and Peggy Cope
Terry Cork
Eric and Gwenda Cornish
Brenda and Kenneth Cornwell

Brian Cox
Geoff Cox
Rosemary Cox
Ian Crawshaw
Carolyn and Jack Davenport
Edward John Davies
Irene Margaret Davies
Mr. and Mrs. R.J. Davis
Councillor Alan L. Day
Chris and Sam Day
Maurice Dedman
Clive Dellow
Sonja and Haydn Delve
Robert and Caroline Derriman
Mary Jane Divino
The Doheny Family
Simon, Lynda and Keith Donan
Janice Dowd
Birgit van Driel
Rutger van Driel
Dr. Eric Duckworth
Robert Bryn Duncan
Mrs. Eileen Dyer
Bill Eastwell
Mr. and Mrs. Michael
   Edmondson
Don and Betty Edwards
Greta Edwards
Anne Egleton
Susan Egleton
Trevor Egleton
Doreen Elderfield
Mr. E.J. Elderfield (Ted)
Gerald W. Elderfield
Mrs. Joan Elderfield
Robert Elderfield
Tony Elderfield
Mrs. Jane Elliot (née Elderfield)
Moira and John Elliott
June Elsworth
Jacqueline Esling
George and Lena Evered
Mrs. G.J. Farr
Mr. and Mrs. G.R. Farren
Sally Farrow
Rob Fear
Gill and Mike Field
Mr. John Field
Kurt Fleet

Revd. David Flower
Freddie Fordham
Harry Fordham
Revd. J. Robin E. Fox
Andy French
Joan Fuller
Chris Furness
Nancy Galatola
Mr. W.T. Gale
Maida and Alistair Gardner
Iris and Keith Garrett
Pamela Gay
Alan and Barbara Geany
Fred Gibson
Roger Gill
A.W. Gillham
Victor H. Gillham
Phyllis Gould
Mrs. Carol A. Green
Mr. and Mrs. James Green
Tony and Eileen Green
Annette Greenough
Tony and Pamela Hadaway
Gill, Peter and Ben Halls
Keith and Iris Hamilton
David Hampshire
Tim Hanson
Vic and Jeanette Harasimow
Mrs. Hilda Hardy
Revd. C.E. Harris, JP
Steve J. Harris
Mrs. E. Harrod (née Bunby)
F.A.P.N. and M. Harrod
Ned Hartley, M.B.E.
Trevor Harvey
Michael and Sybil Hastings
Jeff and Sadie Hatcher
Christopher Hawes
Cliff and Sheila Hayward
Michael George Hayward
Arthur Hazell
Jack Hearne
Mrs. J.B. Higgins
John E. Hobbs
Tim and Kate Holliday
Jill Holmes
Heather and Jon Homan
Chris Hood
Marion and David Horn
Vanessa and Gillian Horn
Andrée Welstead Hornby
Joseph Hornby
Ruth and Ray Horver
The Hosking Family

David J.V. Hoskins
Joseph William Howe
Ann and Nick Hoyle
Gillian M. Hubble
Ian and Heather Huntley
Joan and Colin Hurt
ICI Paints
Gilbert R. Ireland
J.T. Ireland, C.B.E.
Sidney H. Ireland
Keith Iveson
Wendy Jacobs
Douglas James
Jack James
Mrs. Margaret James
Dennis and Ann Jeffries
Freddie Johnson
G. and L.J. Johnson-Taylor
Henry and the late Hilda Jolley
Mr. and Mrs. A. Jones
Richard Josebury
K. and J. Joslin
Mrs. Valerie Kayl
Deborah M. Kelly
William Kennard, O.B.E., I.S.O.
Irene Evelyn Kennedy
John and Claire Kernot
Karen Kershaw and Russell
    West and Family
Mrs. Doreen Kersley
I.J. Kilby
Zoe Kitching
David Kneller
Mr. Konishi and Family
Mrs. Mary Lamb (née
    Elderfield)
Ann Learmont (Easson Family)
Mr. and Mrs. Martin D. Lee
Anthony P. Levings
Rex Lingham-Wood
D.A. Lipscombe
Chris Livesley
Mrs. E. Lockwood
Don Lunn
John and Jean Lunt
B. Lyford
J. Lyford
M. Lyford
Iain Mackenzie
David and Sally Mackey
Dr. Peter H. Mackie
Bob and Joy Maddock
Mrs. Rachael Mankiewicz (née
    Elderfield)

Jill and Paul Martindale
G.S. Mathews
Professor and Mrs. C.J. Mathias
Charles Maxwell
Edna Mayer
John and Penny Mayhew
Margaret McCormick
Cliff S. McCorry
Mrs. Beena Menon
R.C. Meyer
Ted and Ann Meyer
Peter and Anne Milne
Cyril Milne-Smith
Gordon and Betty Milne-Smith
Michael and Patricia Milne-Smith
Mr. D. Mitchell
Mr. G.C. and Mrs. C.A. Montague
Nick Moore
Louise J. Morgan
Ken Morris
Evelyn Morrison
Mrs. Marion Morrison
L.M. Mortin
Mr. and Mrs. K. Moss
Mum
Alan and Debbie Munro
Frederick Charles Murphy
Dr. and Mrs. H. Nakahara
Nan
P.R. Neville
R.W. and B.A. New
Roy J. Nichols
Joyce Noble
Daphne E. Norcross
Mrs. Jill Norman
Katie, Amy and Heather Oliver
Graham M. O'Loughlin
Mr. Katsuhiko Omaru and
    Family
Geoff Orange
Richard J.J. Orton
Vera Oversby
L. Paine (née Shillabeer)
Mr. W.H. Paine
Brian and Sheena Pardoe
Stanley and Mary Parr
Thos W. Parratt
Andrew and Nicky Parry
Kathryn Pate
Marian Payne
Miss Joyce M. Pellant
Edward Roy Pelling
Samantha Jane Pelling
Tim Penfold

Jack Pepper
Peter Perman
Pioneer GB Limited
Michael Pitfield
Harry Ponton
Mrs. Jean Porter
E.K. Price
Doreen Prior
Jean Prior
K. and G.H. Pugh
Harold, Jane and Hilda Rabbitt
Janice Rangecroft
Cecil A. Redfern
David Redmond
Roger and Pamela Reed
Francisca and Philip Rees
Stanley Reeves
Katie, Mark and Jacob Relf
P.M. Relf
S.W. Relf
The Rice Family
Valerie Richards (Farrow)
John Riley
G. Philip Rimington
David J. Robertson
Sheina Robertson
Mrs. Joyce Robinson (née Wilkins)
Lynda M. Robinson
Mr. G.E. Rogers
Mrs. Valerie Rogers
R.J. and A.M. Rosenthal
Mrs. Maureen E. Rowntree
Douglas D. Roxburgh
Rodney Royston C.C.
Margaret Rudge
Alan Ryman
Alec Ryman
Cissie Lucretia Ryman
Mr. Akihito Sato and Family
Mr. J.R. Scott
Maureen Joan Sellwood
Mrs. Betty Senior (née James)
Alistair Douglas Granville Sharp (Easson Family)
J. Michael Sheasby
D. Shillabeer

Alan and Caroline Shuttleworth
Ann Simner
Steven Simner
Dee Simons
Norman and Ruth Skinner
Robert Slater
N.G.J. Smelt
Graham Geoffrey Smith
Jo, Paul, Alex and Ellie Smith
Mr. and Mrs. Grahaeme Smyth
The Spencer and Webster Families
Phyllis M. Stainer
The Stallwood Family
Vivian Stannett
Michael Stanton
Michael and Jenny Stephenson
Dr. E. Stielow
Patricia (Paddy) Stock
Neil D. Stone
Joan Swift
Norman Swift
The Symonds Family
Philip and Audrey Tarrant
Mr. and Mrs. A. Taylor
Angela Taylor
Bryan and Kathleen Thompson (née Evans)
Shauna, Rowena and Mark Thompson
Alf and Joyce Tindell
Judy Tipping
The Tomey Family
Barbara Tomlinson
G.J. Took
Debbie Towart
Gavin Towart
Lachlan Towart
Rob Towart
The Towart Family
B. and C. Travess
Miss A.M. Tuddenham
Jennifer and Hugh Tulloch
Roland and Caroline Turner
John and Pauline Upton
B.C. Varley
Donald Vincent

R.S.M. Virden
George and Jane Wall
Brian, Lorraine, Philip and Steve Warren
Joanne Watson
Andrew Webb
Kathie Webber
Inez Webster
R.L. Webster
Margaret and Peter Welch
Police Sergeant Tony Welch
Anne Weller
Jacqueline Weller
Nigel Weller
The Welsh Family
Roy and Tracie Welsh and Family
Joan Wells
Mr. A.G. and Mrs. M.D.G. Westwood
Moira White
Rob and Cindy White
Mr. and Mrs. M.K. Whitehouse
Ann Whiting
Stephen L. Whitley
Jacob and Edward Whittaker
Mr. H.S. Whittam
Mr. and Mrs. P.C.A. Wilkinson
The Williams Family
Joan Williams
Roy Leighton Williams
Cyril Wilson
Mrs. Doreen D. Wilson
Frank Wiltshire
Doreen Wing
David and Vivien Wood
F.O. Jon Wood
Mrs. J.G. Wood
Nanette Woodbridge
Jennifer M. Woolveridge
Julia Worms
Alan Wright
Stephen Wright
William Wright
Mr. and Mrs. Stuart Young
Tony and Julie Young

Introduction

One thousand years may be only the blink of an eye in geological time, but it remains an enormous time span in the life of man, equal to 33 generations of those people who have lived, worked and died to make Stoke Poges the unique community that it is today. Lionel Rigby and his fellow contributors, Elizabeth Waghorn, Trevor Harvey, Mike Milne-Smith, Ian Huntley and Frank Bowater are to be congratulated on their efforts in researching material for this unique record of the people and events which would otherwise lie forgotten in archives and record offices across the country. Old buildings can be seen in an entirely new light when their history is known and the people associated with them revealed.

From the time of Domesday Book to the present the community has developed from a completely self-sufficient group of some 70 people to the present inhabitants who are wholly dependent on the goods and services supplied from beyond the parish boundaries.

Looking more closely at the people in this narrative all human nature is to be seen, from the shameful behaviour of Baron de Molyns to the philanthropy of Edward Hastings, and the later work of the Reverend Sidney Godolphin Osborne. The reader can follow the development of social care from the Elizabethan poor laws administered by the Parish through to the development of poor houses and the eventual transfer of care of the poor and the elderly to the larger district union of workhouses or hospitals.

Throughout the narrative the Church and Manor House have remained closely linked both physically and administratively. It is surprising that the Church of St Giles, which has remained in the same place for over 1,000 years, should be so distant from the community it serves. We know from history that the Almshouse and the Vicarage were removed at the whim of an occupant of the Manor House, but were other buildings removed as well? Finally, we must remember the famous poet Thomas Gray and his 'Elegy in a Country Churchyard' which has brought Stoke Poges out of obscurity. This haunting poem recalls the pace of rural life that is lost forever. We must as a community remain vigilant to the threat of wholesale redevelopment of the land that earlier generations have tried to protect in order to retain its rural nature.

Dr. Charles Mobbs FRCGP
Lord of the Manor of Stoke Poges

One
The Origin of the Name 'Stoke Poges'

The earliest known owner of the manor of Stoke and Ditton was Sired the Saxon, vassal of Harold. Following the Norman Conquest, Sired was dispossessed and William Fitz-Ansculf, who came from Picardy, was given the manor as tenant *in capite*—that is direct from the Crown. William had little personal connection with his manor of 'Stoches Ditton', being lord of 16 manors in Buckinghamshire, 12 in Berkshire and 68 elsewhere, while his principal seat was at Dudley in Worcestershire. His daughter Beatrice married Fulk Paganall. This family, from whom Newport Pagnell derives its name, held Stoche Ditton until the end of the 12th century when Hawse Paganall married John de Somerie. The de Somerie family held it for eight generations until 1322. The last reference to the lordship was in 1438.

We are more concerned with Fitz-Ansculf's tenant Walter named in Domesday Book in 1086. The entry reads:

> Walter also holds STOKE (Poges) from William. It answers for 10 hides. Land for 10 ploughs; in lordship 2.
>
> 10 villagers with 3 smallholders have 6 ploughs; a further 2 possible.
>
> 4 slaves; 1 mill at 4s; woodland, 500 pigs. Total value £5; when acquired £3; before 1066 £6.
>
> Sired, Earl Harold's man, held this manor; he could sell. A Freeman, Tubbi's man, held 1 hide of this land; he could sell.

A hide was a measurement used for tax assessment. It was the amount of land a single family needed to support itself. The acreage was variable depending on the quality of the land and was usually from 100 to 120 acres. The woodland was the most extensive in Buckinghamshire since it provided sufficient acorns to keep 500 pigs. Villagers and smallholders were the upper and lower grades of peasantry. The 10 villagers, 3 smallholders and

1 Norman warrior.

4 bondmen or slaves, in all 17 men, formed a population of perhaps 70 when women and children were added.

The descendants of Walter, who were the tenants from 1086 to 1291, took the name de Stoke, or Stoches in Domesday Book, thus more closely associating themselves with the manor. The word Stoke derives from an Anglo-Saxon root meaning 'the place'. There are a number of other Stokes in England. Probably, in each instance, the name was given to the first considerable house, possibly stockaded, in a sparsely occupied area. By degrees the title given to the house would be given to the manor also, and become the name of its possessors with the prefix 'de' (of) as in Hugh de Stoke.

The Saxon meaning of Stoke as 'a place' could also link it to the Hundred Court whose meeting place was Stoke. The shires were divided into hundreds and at this time Buckinghamshire had 18 including Stoke Hundred. Originally hundreds were the areas occupied by a hundred families but they later became groups of manors or villages. The Hundred Court met every month and dealt with private pleas, criminal and taxation matters. The exact site in Stoke where it met is not known. Representatives of the local villages had to walk to Stoke to attend, and the tracks made by these and other journeys are probably the origin of Wexham Road from Upton and Ditton and Stoke Poges Lane from Chalvey.[1] Each manor also had a manorial court to adjudicate on minor misdemeanours.

About the year 1107 Hugh de Stoke and his wife joined with Aluredus (Alfred), the priest of Stoke, to make over the church and tithes of Stoke and Ditton for ever to the Priory of St Mary Overy in Southwark. The Charter was witnessed by William Gifford, Bishop of Winchester. By presenting the church to the Priory of St Mary, Hugh de Stoke exercised the rights he or his family must have enjoyed as founder. Of this early building only the north wall of the chancel remains. There are recorded references to the de Stoke family. In 1199 Thomas de Stoke was one of the parties in a legal transaction concerning lands in Stoke, and there is a mention of a Sir Roger de Stoke.

In the 13th century Richard de Stoke held the manor and was still living in 1242. In 1254 Humbert or Imbert de Pogeis or Pugeys had custody of Stoke as guardian of Amicia de Stoke, the daughter and heiress of Richard de Stoke. Imbert Pogeis came to England in 1236 with Eleanor of Provence when she married Henry III. Imbert became steward of King Henry III's household between 1257 and 1262. The family probably owed their name to the village Poges on the coast of

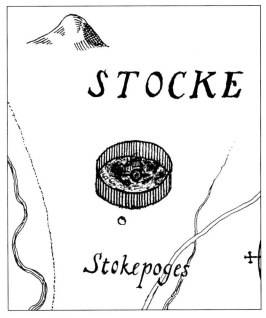

2 An illustration of the origin of 'Stoke', possibly by John Speed.

3 In 1968 villages mentioned in Domesday Book were asked to fix commemorative plaques on a suitable building. The Stoke Poges plaque was placed on the wall of the Hastings Chapel of St Giles' Church. The Reverend Cyril Harris, Lionel Rigby and Ned Hartley are standing underneath the plaque and holding the Buckinghamshire Domesday Book entries. (*Slough Observer* photograph.)

Normandy near where the Black Prince was knighted before the Battle of Crecy. Imbert's son Robert married Amicia de Stoke sometime before 1291. Over a period of time the name Poges became associated with Stoke.

Two
The de Molyns Family

Robert and Amicia Poges had two sons, Peter and Thomas, and two daughters, Margaret and Eleanor. Peter married and had a son John. In November 1326 robbers broke into the manor house at Stoke and slew Peter and his small son, making off with money and valuables. Robert Poges died in his 80s, his other son and two daughters having predeceased him, and his heirs were his three granddaughters. One of the granddaughters, Egidia or Gill, the daughter of Margaret Poges by her marriage to Sir John Mauduit, inherited the manor in 1331. The other two had quit-claimed or relinquished their interest to John de Molyns whom Egidia had married in 1325. The evidence suggests that this had been done under duress. In July 1330 John de Molyns was indicted for aiding and abetting the murder of Peter Poges, his son and the family cook. Although a jury of the Stoke Hundred acquitted him of this crime Molyns was charged in 1340 with thwarting the course of justice and in effect using his influence to fix the jury.

Having the heiress of Stoke as his wife gave John a good start on his remarkable rise to power 'but the obvious factor which turned him into one of the wealthiest men in Buckinghamshire and one of the most important men in England later on was his own forceful personality and great ability. His early career belongs to the reign of Edward II. The few glimpses we have of him suggest an ambivalent line of political conduct, a necessary prerequisite [sic] for survival in the terrible days of the civil war followed by the Despenser regime'.[1]

The Despensers were a powerful faction supporting Edward II. He was a weak monarch confronted by powerful barons. In 1326 Edward's queen, Isabella, invaded England and the Despensers were hunted down and killed. Edward was murdered in Berkeley Castle. The new king,

Edward III, was only 14 and Isabella ruled England with her lover Roger Mortimer.

Molyns had an important patron in William Montague, later to become Earl of Salisbury, who served Edward III in his break away from his mother Queen Isabella and Mortimer. Molyns took part in the coup at Nottingham Castle in October 1330 which led to the execution of Mortimer and banishment of Isabella. Montague was rewarded with an earldom by the young king and Molyns also earned royal favour. Thus began the spectacular rise of Molyns in the service of his king as squire, knight and, in 1337, banneret of the royal household. This last honour, being a higher form of knighthood, was usually awarded for valour in the field of battle.

Molyns undertook a variety of commissions for Edward III including one to survey the Tower of London, implying a considerable knowledge of fortifications. He also received a royal licence to fortify his manor houses at Stoke and Ditton and to enclose three woods to form Stoke Park. Within parks deer would be hunted for pleasure and to provide a supply of venison; outside parks all deer belonged to the king. Molyns acquired some twenty additional manors in different parts of the country but mostly in Buckinghamshire. Valuable rights were also conferred on him with charters, the right to hold fairs and other royal grants, all of which generated income. In 1331 he rebuilt the nave of St Giles and refounded the church, he and his wife obtaining a charter empowering him to hold a fair on St Giles' Day. The tomb in the north wall of the chancel, in the form of an Easter Sepulchre, is said to be Sir John's.

Not only had he become wealthy, but he also had connections with London merchants, the source of loans the king needed for his part in the early stages of the Hundred Years War with France. This led to Sir John's first fall from favour in 1340. The king had abandoned the siege of Tournai through lack of funds. Amongst others, Molyns was arrested for rebellion and sent to the Tower. Other charges included abuses and infringement of law and order in Buckinghamshire. The king inaugurated an inquiry into the conduct of corrupt officials and the charges against Molyns were serious, including criminal offences against his own family, murder, subverting a justice of the King's Bench to escape detection, terrorism in Buckinghamshire and illegal appropriation of land. The king proceeded to seize the valuables and other goods of Molyns. On 4 December 1340 the king rode out to St Albans and, with the abbot not daring to resist him, he had the locks forced on the room containing the Molyns' treasure. After Christmas the king went to Ditton and took a great quantity of silver and plate, and armour sufficient for 80 men. The king then went to Stoke where he and his friends spent three days feasting and carousing. The list of goods seized included an invalid chair, probably that of Robert Poges.

Sir John escaped from the Tower, failed to present himself to answer charges and was outlawed. In 1345 he received a royal pardon and his lands were restored. In 1346-7 he served with the king in France on the Crecy campaign. He was summoned as a magnate to the great council of 1347 giving his descendants the right to be summoned as peers. In 1352 Queen Philippa made him steward of her household. Within two years the queen became dissatisfied as he sought to profit from his office and in 1357 he fell from favour for a second time. He and his wife were charged with 'treasons, felonies, robberies, conspiracies and confederations'. The Buckinghamshire jurors presented a formidable dossier against Sir John. The charges for which he was convicted and imprisoned for felony even included stealing the vicar of Stoke Poges' horse and that he had, on two separate occasions, given refuge to two murderers. Incarcerated initially in Nottingham Castle, where his career had started, he was later transferred to Cambridge, where he died in 1361 aged about 62. His wife, Egidia, was pardoned, dying five years later.

'Amidst all the charges of official corruption which the royal inquiry of 1340 revealed, Molyns' case is unique. No other magnate appears who has terrorised his part of the world for such a length of time. On the other hand, the king's renewed favour towards him after 1346 does not give a reassuring view of the attitude of King Edward and his wife to disorderly and over-mighty subjects.'[2]

Sir John de Molyns was succeeded by his son William who died in 1380. William was succeeded by his son Richard de Molyns who died four years later in 1384, having been captured by the Scots in 1382 and forced to fell his timber at Stoke Poges to pay for his ransom. Richard's son William, 1377/8-1425, was married before Michaelmas 1405 to Margery or Margaret. The two brasses in St Giles within the altar rail on the south side are of Sir William and his wife. The brass of Sir William shows him in full armour with sword and dagger.

His heir was also called William and he was born in Stoke Poges and baptised in St Giles' Church on 8 December 1405. At his christening he received a white horse from his godfather William Wyot, a fine, very valuable sword from his other godfather William Kingston, Dean of Windsor, and from his godmother a hawk. He was killed in 1429 defending a bridge from a French sortie at the siege of Orleans. He was the last male de Molyns and he left a daughter Alianore or Eleanor as his heiress. She was born in 1426 at Stoke Poges and was therefore three years of age when her father died.

There is a record of an inquisition held in Colnbrook in 1440, probably in consequence of Eleanor's marriage to Sir Robert Hungerford, to prove her age. Twelve witnesses to her baptism

Ḧr iačt ŵilłius ǥolǳus ařịłcs qui obįt ḷmị ḍur exeẇṫ Ịẇiȷ Ị°
ǒm ǚ ḉ ḉ ḉ ḉ rrv° Śt ḍẅa ṁaịrịa ṿ͗ eḷ ǵ͗ aŵḃᵣṗẇr͗ ḍr̓ aṁē

were examined on oath and from their testimony we learn that her godmothers were Alice, Countess of Salisbury, and Elizabeth, Lady Say. The former, who wore a robe of gold at the baptism, gave the child a cup with a gold cover; the latter, who wore a gown of pale blue damask, gave her a silver gilt basin and ewer. The child's godfather, Thomas, Lord Skales, who wore a gown of pale blue velvet, gave her £20. A basin and ewer of silver gilt were carried from the manor house to the church for the godparents to wash their hands in after the ceremony, and two silver gilt bowls containing wine of 'ypocras and clarrey' (a cordial drink made of wine flavoured with spices) were provided for the guests in the church.[3] Eleanor is buried in St Giles' Church on the south side of the altar rails, but the slab is without her effigy and only the inscription remains, recording her marriages, first to Lord Hungerford and secondly to Sir Oliver Manningham.

Three

The Hungerford and Hastings Families

Alianore or Eleanor de Molyns was aged 15 years in 1441 when she married Sir Robert Hungerford, who thereafter took her title and was called Lord Hungerford and Molyns. This was during the reign of Henry VI when the country was exhausted and overtaxed and in the final stages of the Hundred Years War with France. Justice was manipulated by the nobles and when, in 1451, Lord Hungerford was indicted for an armed attack on the Manor of Gresham, the Sheriff of Norfolk received 'writing from the Kyng that he shall make a panell to acquyte the Lord Moleyns', and acquitted he was. Hungerford, who was in dispute with John Paston over the ownership of the manor, had sent a thousand men to dislodge him. Eventually, ownership was conceded to Paston.

In 1453 Hungerford was captured by the French at the Battle of Castillon. Seven years later he was released on payment of a ransom of £3,000 and Stoke Poges manor formed part of the security for this sum. On his return in 1460 as compensation for this misfortune he was granted a licence to export 1,500 sacks of wool without payment of duty. At this time wool and cloth were England's most important exports and custom duties were charged on exported goods.

Meanwhile, the country was divided by the Wars of the Roses and Hungerford fought with the Lancastrians when they were defeated at the Battle of Towton Field in 1461. He fled with the king to Scotland. Declared a traitor and attainted[1] in Edward IV's first parliament, he rallied the

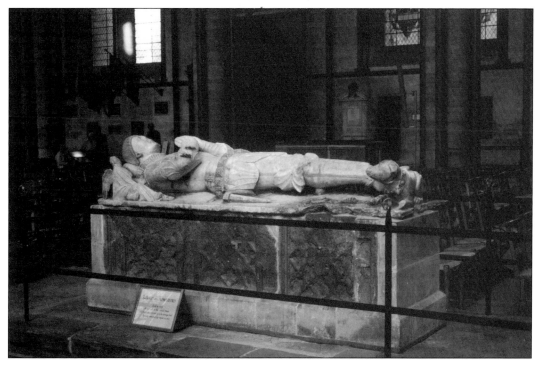

5 Robert Lord Hungerford's alabaster effigy in Salisbury Cathedral. (Reproduced by permission of the Dean and Chapter.)

6 The yew tree in the churchyard of St Giles, *c.*1915.

7 George Hastings (1488-1545), 1st Earl of Huntingdon and 3rd Baron Hastings of Hastings. He died in Stoke Poges and is buried in the chancel of St Giles. (Painting attributed to Ambrosius Benson, copright IRPA-KIK, Brussels.)

Lancastrians in the north of England. He was captured by the Yorkists in 1464 after the defeat of the Lancastrians at the Battle of Hexham. Executed as a traitor at Newcastle, he is buried in Salisbury Cathedral. Robert Hungerford's son Thomas was also attainted and was executed by Edward IV in 1469 leaving his daughter Mary, then aged 11 years, as his heiress.

Mary was placed in the wardship of her grandmother Eleanor, and later this was transferred to William Lord Hastings. Hastings arranged a marriage covenant which stipulated that she should marry Edward his eldest son 'or in the event of her refusing or his dying, to Richard another son or in like case to George another son'. In Shakespeare's *King Henry the Sixth Part 3* the Duke of Clarence says ironically: 'For this one speech Lord Hastings well deserves/To have the heir of the Lord Hungerford'.

William Lord Hastings was put to death by Richard III but the victory of Henry Tudor at

Bosworth in 1485 reversed the fortunes of the Hastings family. In the same year the estate at Stoke, which had been forfeit to the Crown, was restored to Mary, who had married Sir Edward Hastings in 1480, the attainders on her father and grandfather having been reversed in her favour.

Two years before the Battle of Bosworth a statute decreed a general planting of yew to increase the supply of suitable wood for military bows, most bows at that time being imported. The yew in St Giles' churchyard probably dates from this time.[2]

Mary and Edward had a son George, who was a faithful servant of Henry VIII, and was created the 1st Earl of Huntingdon in 1529. He signed the letter to Clement VII which warned the Pope of the consequences of a refusal to grant Henry a divorce from Catherine of Aragon. George was also one of the 26 peers whose judgement condemned Anne Boleyn to the block in 1536. He died in 1545.

The occupants of the Stoke Poges Manor House again faced the peril of choice. The two brothers who chose opposite sides were the sons of George: Francis the 2nd Earl and his brother Edward. On the death of Edward VI, Francis joined in the proclamation of Lady Jane Grey as queen. Mary Tudor addressed a very urgent letter to Edward, exhorting him to suppress the tumults that had arisen in Buckinghamshire in favour of her rival. Edward zealously answered her call and, raising a body of 4,000 men in the county, succeeded in establishing the interests of Mary. Perhaps it was the influence of his brother that saved Francis from the Tower, but he quickly atoned for his error by his support for the new queen. Edward was liberally rewarded with the Garter and a peerage when he became Lord Hastings of Loughborough.

Both brothers left their mark on Stoke Poges. Francis completed the building of the Manor House in 1555, five years before he died. The magnificent Tudor building, of which only one wing now remains, probably replaced the fortified house of de Molyns. Edward built the Hastings Chapel on to St Giles' Church and, in 1557, the last year of Mary's reign, he procured a special Act of Parliament to enable him to found a hospital or almshouse in Stoke Poges. He died without issue in 1573 and is buried in the Hastings Chapel.

8 Water-colour etching, dated 1804, of the Manor House before all but the west wing was demolished. The existing building was gifted to the District Council by the Mobbs Memorial Trust in 1971.

Four
The Hastings Chapel and Almshouse

Before the Reformation wealthy people often left money to endow chantries so that prayers could be offered for their souls. After the Reformation the Protestant Church did not favour this practice and an alternative was the founding of hospitals or almshouses which combined the object of a chantry with accommodation for the poor, part of whose duties would be to say prayers for the founder.

The almshouse built by Lord Hastings housed four poor men and two poor women. Every two years each resident received four yards of cloth for a gown on the sleeve of which was the crest of their benefactor, a bull's head. The men could be 'sole or married' but the women were to be 'sole and unmarried'. After the death of Lord Hastings the brethren and sisters, as they were to be known, were elected by the Vicar of Stoke and five substantial men of the parish. It was the inmates' duty to 'repair daily to the church, to hear God's service, and also to pray for the souls aforesaid'.

The almshouse was built on the south side of the church and the inmates were allowed to graze six cows in the adjoining Stoke Park. Lord Hastings must have felt that future owners of the Manor might not take too kindly to having the almshouse nearby with its right to pasture six cows. He therefore obtained an indenture to confirm this right to pasture.

Some two hundred years later Thomas Penn decided it was inconvenient to have the hospital and grounds adjoining his property and their cows

9 The Hastings Almshouse, Park Road, Stoke Poges in 1892. (The Wilder Collection.)

10 The Hastings Almshouse in 1999, now a private residence known as The Clock House.

11 A window depicting Lord Hastings of Loughborough, which could have been in St Giles during the 17th or early 18th centuries. Its present location is unknown.

grazing in his park. In order to move the hospital to a new location Penn was required to obtain a further Act of Parliament which he did in 1765. The old almshouse or hospital was demolished and re-built in Park Road, opposite Gray's Meadow. There it remained in use until it was sold in 1947 by the then trustees. The almshouse was in a bad state of repair and it was hoped that replacement almshouses could be built in the adjoining Hastings Meadow. Post-war planning legislation prevented development on what became part of the green belt and no replacement almshouses were built. The former almshouse is now a private residence known as the Clock House.

There had been a third Act of Parliament in 1856 which vested the Trust in a Scheme of the Charity Commission. The proceeds of the 1947 sale remained invested and, in 1980, after a protracted series of negotiations over a number of years with the Charity Commission, an Order was laid before Parliament for a new scheme to widen the objectives of the Trust. The new order, called the Charities (Lord Hastings Hospital Trust) Order 1980,

was approved by resolution of each House of Parliament. Again, as in 1765, this was necessary because the Trust had been established by Act of Parliament.

The old almshouse trust might have been merged into a larger almshouse charity with minimal connections with Stoke Poges but for the insistence of the then trustees for a new and updated scheme for Stoke Poges. The Charity Commission required a search for a new site to provide accommodation in Stoke Poges before agreeing to preparation of a new scheme, whereby the money for almshouses could be invested and the interest used to relieve the poor in other ways. No site was found.

The new scheme provides for eight trustees of whom one is the vicar of the parish ex officio, one is nominated by the parish council and the other six are co-optative trustees. Although the trustees retain the power to provide almshouses, they now have further powers for helping residents in the Parish of Stoke Poges who are in need, hardship or distress.

Five

Sir Edward Coke, the Great Lawyer

The last of the Hastings family to own the Manor was Henry, the 3rd Earl of Huntingdon. He was influential at the Court of Elizabeth I and was entrusted with the task of guarding Mary, Queen of Scots. Henry was compelled to mortgage the Manor House because of his financial difficulties and when he died in 1595 he was so poor that Queen Elizabeth paid his funeral expenses. Ownership passed to Sir Edward Coke in 1596 although it is said to have been occupied by Sir Christopher Hatton, a favourite of the Queen. Thomas Gray gives credence to this in his poem 'The Long Story'.

Sir Edward Coke, the great lawyer, lived at the Manor House until his death. He entertained Queen Elizabeth there with much pomp and ceremony in 1601 and presented her with jewels to the value of £1,200. As attorney general from 1594, Coke conducted the prosecution of Essex,

Raleigh and the Gunpowder Conspirators. More notable were his writings codifying the Common Law—his Reports (1600-15, 1650-9) and his Institutes (1628-44). Some of these works were not published until after his death. In 1606 Coke became Chief Justice of the Common Pleas and championed the Common Law against the attempts by James I to exalt the royal prerogative. He was Lord Chief Justice of England from 1613 to 1617 and a reluctant High Sheriff of Buckinghamshire in 1625. This latter crown appointment was used by Charles I to debar Coke from sitting in the House of Commons during his year of office. Later, in 1628, he drew up the Petition of Right to curb the king's power. The Petition asked for 'recognition of a claim that every subject of the Crown had been wronged in certain specific matters, and that, in future, the law should be observed'. Coke died before Charles I's conflict with Parliament led to the Civil War.

When he died at the age of 82 in 1634, Sir Edward felt himself 'alone on earth, deserted by his friends and detested by his wife'. As he lay dying the king's officers were searching his house for seditious papers. Coke's unhappy domestic life had resulted from his second marriage to a wealthy widow much younger than himself, Lady Elizabeth Hatton. She died 11 years after Coke. In her will she left two bequests, each of £100, one to the Hastings Hospital and the other 'for the reliefe and maintenance of the most sickely and impotent people of the said parish of Stoake'. If there were no such poor then the rent from the land purchased for the sum of £100 was to be used and 'given to maidservants and manservants which have served seaven yeares or so togeather in any one service within the said parish'.

12 Sir Edward Coke (1552-1634).

13 Sir Edward Coke's monument in Stoke Park by James Wyatt, 1800. The Roman Doric column is 58 feet high with the statue of Sir Edward by Rossi.

14 Sir Edward Coke's monument, close-up of Rossi's statue.

Land of some fourteen acres was purchased in Wexham, known as Poor's Field and, since there were always poor in need, the alternative use as marriage portions never arose. Poor's Field is still owned by Stoke United Charities and because of gravel extraction it has now invested in excess of £100,000. Whilst we remember Lady Hatton in Stoke Poges as a benefactress, Sir Edward Coke is also commemorated. In 1800 John Penn commissioned the architect James Wyatt to erect a memorial column in Stoke Park. The fluted Roman Doric column is 58 feet high and carries a statue of Coke by Rossi.

Dr. W.O. Hassall of the Bodleian Library, who was curator to Lord Leicester, a descendant of Coke, wrote to him in 1966 when the monument was in need of repair. An extract reads: 'Sir Edward

Coke's importance in the county of Buckinghamshire is far more than that of being the greatest sheriff that that county ever has had, and the monument is most important for its meaning and significance. I believe this is the only monument of our greatest Lawyer in the home counties. I feel therefore that this is far more than a local, let alone a family matter, for it is a strange chance that the monument of the greatest champion of constitutional processes and freedom from dictatorship should stand near Runnymede. Coke's monument marks the home in which when he lay dying, the enemies of the common law searched his papers for seditious matter.'

It is of interest to note that Coke's descendants acquired the Holkham estate in Norfolk, built Holkham Hall and became Earls of Leicester. One of them, Coke of Norfolk, with his scientific approach to agriculture, became one of the great pioneers of the Agricultural Revolution. In the first half of the 19th century this led to improvements in productivity essential at that time to feed the growing population of England.

Six

The Owners of the Manor House from 1640 to 1760

Sir Edward Coke arranged the marriage of his second daughter to Sir John Villiers, later Viscount Purbeck. This was against her will and the wishes of Lady Hatton her mother. Villiers was the brother of the Duke of Buckingham, a favourite of King Charles I. Sir Edward hoped that this alliance would help him to regain the King's favour. He is said to have shut up his wife and daughter, 14-year-old Frances, in the Manor House until the latter consented to the marriage. This and other incidents made for a stormy relationship.

The estate passed to Viscount Purbeck when Lady Hatton died in 1644. It was in 1647, during his ownership, that King Charles I was imprisoned in the Manor House whilst being taken to London. It is recorded in Whitelock's memorials: 'Aug. 2nd The Army quartered at Colnebrooke, and the King at Stoke Abby' and 'Aug. 15th From the Army

15 Wall painting of armorial bearings in the Manor House said to be the work of Charles I. It shows the ragged staff, with two bears, within a garter on which is the Royal motto, surmounted with a coronet; beneath are the initials E.B.

we had further this day, that the King removed Friday from Stoke House'.

In 1656 the Manor passed to the Gayer family, first to John Gayer and then to his brother Robert. Robert Gayer, loyal to the Stuarts, was created a Knight's Companion of the Order of the Bath at the coronation of King Charles II. In 1688, soon after he ascended the throne, William III visited Stoke and, passing the Manor House, expressed a wish to see it. But Sir Robert Gayer, in spite of his wife's entreaties, stoutly refused him admission. 'He has got possession of another man's house', he said, 'and he shall not enter mine,' and the king, who was actually standing outside the gate, had to depart. Sir Robert died in 1702 and was succeeded by his eldest son, also called Robert, who sold the estate in 1724 to Edmund Halsey for the sum of £12,000. Halsey's daughter Anne married Sir Richard Temple who was created Viscount Cobham in 1718. The Cobhams owned Stowe as well as Stoke and, when Viscount Cobham died in 1749, Lady Cobham retired to Stoke.

In 1750 a plan for landscaping Stoke was drawn up by Capability Brown, who had been employed by Viscount Cobham to landscape Stowe. Brown's design included linking five quadrangular pools to make a river-like lake and, although this design was not immediately executed, this is the lake now forming the western boundary to the grounds of the Manor House. The conversion of fish ponds into lakes is typical of this period. John Rocque's map of 1761 shows the five ponds. An engraving of a painting by H. Pugh in 1765 of Thomas Penn and his family in front of the old Manor House shows the five ponds converted into a lake.

In the same year, 1750, the incident occurred that led to Thomas Gray writing his poem 'A Long

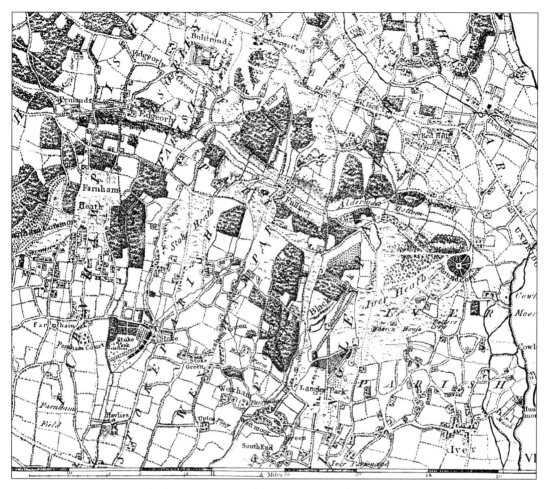

16   Part of John Rocque's map of 1761 showing the five quadrangular pools.

Story'. Gray spent his summer vacations at West End House, Stoke Poges, the home of his widowed aunt, Mrs. Anna Rogers, and her two sisters, Mary Antrobus and Dorothy Gray his mother. He had finalised his 'Elegy written in a Country Churchyard' and the manuscript had been read and admired by Lady Cobham. She sent her relative Miss Henrietta Speed and Lady Schaub, who were her guests, to West End House to invite Gray to the Manor House but he was out. On his return, and having read the note they left, he was obliged to return the visit. This led to his humorous poem 'A Long Story' in which he describes the Manor House. The poem also contains references to other local characters such as the housekeeper at the Manor House, Mrs. Tyack, and the steward, Mr. Groom, both of whom are buried in the southwest corner of the churchyard under the weeping beech.

Seven

Thomas Gray and Stoke Poges

Stoke Poges would be far less well-known today but for Thomas Gray and his 'Elegy'. In his time Stoke Poges was a collection of scattered hamlets stretching as far south as the Bath Road in Slough. A busy highway, with 60 to 80 coaches a day at its peak, Slough was one of the important halts on the road to Bath. Travellers boarded their coaches at one of several inns including the *Crown Inn*, the *White Hart* and the *Windmill Inn* at Salt Hill. Gray travelled extensively over England and Scotland as well as to and from London where he had a house. He would have experienced the discomforts of travel by coach together with the dangers from highwaymen and footpads.

With its open fields, meadows, beechwoods, extensive heathland commons and high-banked winding lanes, Stoke Poges and south Buckinghamshire provided an inspiring setting for the long meditative country walks that so delighted Thomas Gray. Born in Cornhill in 1716, he was the only one of 12 children to survive infancy. His father was an eccentric and violent man so Gray's upbringing and education were left to his long-suffering mother Dorothy Gray. She and her sister, Mary Antrobus, opened a milliner's shop in Cornhill and this enabled Mrs. Gray to support her son at Eton and Cambridge.

Fortunately Dorothy Gray's two brothers, Robert and William Antrobus, were assistant masters at Eton College. In 1725, when Thomas entered Eton, before the age of nine, it was under the care of his uncle Robert. Robert Antrobus lived in Burnham and so Thomas spent his holidays there. Later Dorothy Gray's sister Anna, and her husband Jonathan Rogers, an attorney, retired and settled at Burnham in a house known as Goldwin's at Cant's Hill.

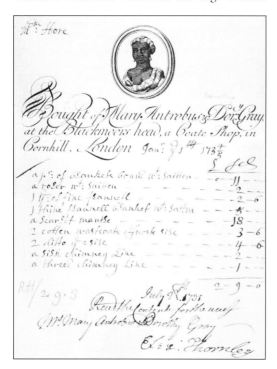

17 An invoice for goods supplied from the Cornhill shop of Mary Antrobus and Dorothy Gray. (By permission of the Trustees of the British Library.)

18 Plaque of Gray at Eton by John Deare. (By permission of the Provost and Fellows of Eton College.)

19 Thomas Gray, from a painting attributed to Jonathan Richardson the elder, but possibly by Arthur Pond. (By permission of the Fitzwilliam Museum, Cambridge.)

20   Gray's pew in the far corner of the south aisle of St Giles.

At Eton, Gray began his friendship with Horace Walpole, Richard West and Thomas Ashton, forming the 'Quadruple Alliance', a little group devoted to literary pursuits. He also gained a love for the literature of Greece and Rome which makes its influence felt in almost every line of his poetry.

21   Gray's Elegy—an engraving of the poet.

We do not know which of his parents commissioned a full-length portrait of their son when he was aged fourteen or fifteen. Although it was attributed to Richardson the Elder, the most fashionable painter of his day, it is possibly by Arthur Pond. It is now in the Fitzwilliam Museum at Cambridge.

In 1735 Walpole and Gray entered Cambridge. Three years later Gray accompanied Walpole on the Grand Tour of Europe but they quarrelled and Gray returned home. Following his return, and his father's death, Gray settled at Peterhouse where he took his degree in law and applied himself to a wide range of study.

Gray spent summer vacations with Jonathan and Anna Rogers, first at Cant's Hill and from 1739 at West End House, Stoke Poges, which Jonathan Rogers leased from the Salter family. For Gray the year 1742 was a significant one. He spent the months of May to October in Stoke Poges where in June he wrote his poem 'Ode on the Spring', recalling the sights and sounds of the Buckinghamshire countryside. He sent the poem to his friend Richard West not knowing that he had died of tuberculosis. Gray responded to this sad news in October with his 'Sonnet on the Death of Mr. Richard West'. In the same month he wrote the 'Ode to Adversity' and the 'Ode on a Distant Prospect of Eton College'. This latter poem contrasts the carefree years of boyhood with the problems of adult life. He also wrote 'Hymn to Ignorance' in 1742.

Jonathan Rogers died in October of that year. Gray's mother and her sister and partner Mary Antrobus wound up the business in Cornhill and moved to Stoke Poges to live with their widowed sister Anna. The association of the poet with Stoke Poges continued for he was a frequent visitor, spending his vacations with his mother, who died in 1753, and with his aunt until she died in 1758. He closed West End House in 1759.

22 On 28 July 1971 the Post Office issued a set of literary anniversary stamps, one of which commemorated the death of Gray in 1771. Stoke Poges had its own first-day covers and cancellation hand stamp for the first day of issue. It also had a hand stamp, dated 30 July 1971, to commemorate the bicentenary of the actual date of Gray's death. The photograph shows a mail coach preparing to leave the village hall. Cliff Hayward and Charlie Hazell hold sacks with the first-day covers and George Smith, the parish clerk, is ready to escort the coach to Slough Post Office via *The Red Lion*, Stoke Green.

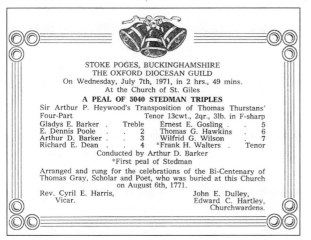

23 A peal of 5,040 Stedman triples was rung by the Stoke Poges ringers on Wednesday 7 July 1971 to honour the poet.

It is said that Gray was most prolific when bereaved. There is evidence to suggest that 1742 was also the year when he started to write his most famous poem, 'Elegy Written in a Country Churchyard'. The 'Elegy' was completed in June 1750 again following a bereavement, that of Mary Antrobus the previous autumn. He sent the completed manuscript to Horace Walpole, writing, 'I have been here at Stoke a few days and having put an end to a thing whose beginning you have seen long ago I immediately send it to you'. Walpole circulated the manuscript amongst his friends. It was not published by Dodsley until the following year. In the meantime, following a visit to the Manor House at Stoke, he wrote 'A Long Story' for Lady Cobham and her guests Lady Schaub and Miss Henrietta Speed.

In 1757 Gray declined the Poet Laureateship and in 1768 was appointed Regius Professor of Modern History at Cambridge. Known as the most learned man in Europe in his day, he died at Cambridge on 30 July 1771. He expressed a desire to be buried 'in a coffin of seasoned oak, neither lined nor covered'. It took two days for his body to reach Stoke Poges. The second night it rested at Salt Hill, Slough, and early the next morning, 6 August 1771, it was deposited in the vault of Dorothy Gray in the churchyard he made famous. In his biography of Thomas Gray, R.W. Ketton-Cremer writes of the Elegy:

It is almost impossible to analyse a work which for two centuries has formed part of the English heritage, so familiar, so constantly quoted, so universally beloved. The exquisite twilight scene with which it opens; the long series of reflections upon fame and obscurity, ambition and destiny; whose stanzas, tolling like solemn bells, which seem to voice all that can be expressed of sadness, resignation and hope—since childhood they have been part of our consciousness, exerting upon us the same irresistible spell as they did upon our forefathers.[1]

Eight
Two Stoke Poges Sailors

John Duckworth was born in 1748 and was six years old when his father Henry Duckworth became Vicar of Stoke Poges. In later life he recalled that he had frequently accompanied his father on visits to Thomas Gray and Mrs. Rogers at West End House. These visits had been returned, and Gray often gave him a shilling or half a crown and this was no inconsiderable present at that time. Following three years at Eton, the young Duckworth entered the Navy at the age of 11 and soon saw action, taking part in the Battle of Quiberon Bay (Brittany, France) in 1759. His naval career was eventful and distinguished although he was under severe criticism at times.

In 1777 he was the 1st lieutenant of a frigate which fired a salute at Rhode Island and accidently killed five men because a shot had been carelessly left in one of the guns. Duckworth and the gunners were court martialled without being named and charged with neglect of duty instead of with causing the deaths of five men. Although they were acquitted, Lord Howe, the Commander in Chief, ordered a new court to be assembled because of the irregularities of the first one. The captains who were summoned to sit on this second court declined to do so 'because the persons charged had been already tried and honourably acquitted'. Howe issued a further order that every captain who persisted in refusing would be suspended from command. The captains thereupon gave nominal obedience by formally meeting and acquitting the accused.

On the outbreak of the French War, Duckworth, as a captain, commanded the *Orion* and took part in the Battle of 1 June 1794. He reached flag rank in 1799 and was knighted in 1801. As a rear admiral in 1805, he faced his second court martial because he had turned a frigate into a

24 Naval officer.

merchant ship and brought home an immense amount of merchandise, thus contravening one of the articles of war. The court martial accepted his explanation that the articles were brought home as presents and not for sale. The matter was raised in Parliament but it was considered that the customs of the service might be held as excusing, if they did not sanction, the irregularities he had certainly committed.

It was on 6 February 1806 that Admiral Sir John Duckworth won a singularly complete victory over the French off St Domingo, when with seven sail of the line he attacked a squadron of five, of which he captured three and destroyed two. His last appointment was as Commander in Chief at Plymouth, just before he died in 1817. A medallion was issued in his honour, the reverse

25 The capture of *L'Amazone* by HMS *Santa Margaretta*, painting by Ralph Dodd. (By permission of the Trustees of the National Maritime Museum.)

of which was inscribed 'Dedicated by his followers to the memory of their illustrious commander'.

During the incumbency of the Reverend Henry Duckworth, another sailor, Captain Elliot Salter, became the owner of West End House. He resided there from 1774 to 1788. Salter presented a petition to the House of Commons in 1784 prompted by an injustice suffered as a result of his humanitarian action in a naval engagement against the French. The petition described the events and the subsequent refusal of the Navy Board to grant a bounty for the capture of a French ship. Two years before, on 29 July 1782, Captain Salter, in command of HMS *Santa Margaretta*, a vessel of 36 guns and

255 men, was cruising off Cape Henry, on the coast of North America, when he sighted a French frigate of equal force to his own ship. At the time, he observed eight large ships, part of a French fleet of 13 sail of the line, bearing down on him. He wore ship (that is he brought his ship about by turning its head away from the wind) and stood from the French frigate, having not only the enemy but a lea shore to encounter. The frigate gave chase until, at about 3 p.m., she made to return to the French fleet which Salter had lost sight of from his masthead except for a second French frigate. Eager to bring the first frigate to an action, Salter judged it proper to tack and stand after her. Within 15 minutes the enemy ship also tacked

and by 5 p.m. the action commenced, lasting for an hour and a quarter and within pistol shot of each other. The French ship, called *L'Amazone*, with some 80 men killed and 70 wounded, surrendered.

Captain Salter sent aboard a lieutenant and a third of his company to take possession of her. The enemy officers and other prisoners were transferred to the *Santa Margaretta*. The situation of *L'Amazone* was critical, her main and mizzen masts over her side, her hull flattened, several guns dismounted and four feet of water in her hold. It was judged most prudent to take her in tow. At daybreak the next morning, the whole French fleet was sighted in chase. Salter recalled his officers and men, cut *L'Amazone* adrift and abandoned his prize. He would have destroyed the enemy ship, but being unable to remove the wounded prisoners he could not bring himself to destroy the ship and them.

According to an Act of Parliament, bounty money was given to naval personnel for the capture or destruction of enemy ships. Captain Salter applied to the Navy Board but his request was refused as the enemy had not been entirely destroyed. In 1784, Salter, after having complied with certain formalities, petitioned the House of Commons. The Journals of the House of Commons, setting out the details of his petition, record that he found it necessary:

to abandon the Prize, which might have been easily destroyed, but not being able to remove the wounded prisoners, his Feelings could not admit of their Destruction, which in that Case must have been inevitable; and that the Petitioner, having applied to the Navy Board for Head Money for the Capture of the above-mentioned Ship, which was in his Possession Twelve Hours, and having received for Answer, that the Act of Parliament did not allow of that Bounty, as the Ship was not entirely destroyed, the Petitioner, in Behalf of himself, his Officers and Ship's Company, finds himself and them entirely precluded from those Advantages, which, he presumes, were intended by the Legislature as an Encouragement to His Majesty's Navy, and to which, under the Spirit of the Act, he conceives his Ship's Company entitled from their Gallantry and very good Conduct on the above mentioned Occasion; And therefore praying the House to take the Premises into Consideration, and grant such Relief as shall appear just and proper.

The petition was referred to a Committee of the House and, subsequently, a Bill was brought in to authorise the payment of the bounty. One can speculate that the Reverend Henry Duckworth and his son John, by this time himself a naval captain, would have discussed naval matters with Captain Salter, and that the progress of Salter's petition to the House of Commons would have been of considerable interest to them both. Surely the vicar would have approved of the humanitarian action which was the cause of the grievance and led to the petition.

Nine

The Penns

On the death of Lady Cobham in 1760 the house and manor were sold to Thomas Penn, Lord Proprietor of the province of Pennsylvania. He was the second son of William Penn, the Quaker who founded the colony of Pennsylvania.

Between 1762 and 1764 Penn carried out general alterations and improvements to the park and grounds from plans by Nathaniel Richmond, a scholar of Capability Brown. He seems to have carried out Brown's earlier landscaping scheme commissioned by Lady Cobham. Penn also moved the Hastings Hospital in 1765 to a new location. This was accomplished only by a special Act of Parliament to empower the necessary exchange of lands. He was then able to improve the view from the Manor House, over the water, to the woods of Langley in the background. The park at the time contained 150 deer. Although there was talk of replacing the Manor House with a new mansion, Stiff Leadbetter was employed to repair the principal suite of rooms called the Great Apartments.

Penn also had a London town house where he kept all his papers relating to Pennsylvania and he expended £3,000 to construct a strong room in it to keep his papers safe. 'Although the Penn papers were never kept at Stoke, it furnished a magnificent setting for an accumulating collection of family portraits by England's best-known artists, and of busts, pastels and miniatures of various Penns and their marital connections,'[1] together with memorabilia of Pennsylvania.

Thomas Penn was buried in St Giles' Church when he died in 1775. By this time the family were no longer Quakers. His estates, including three quarters of the Proprietorial Rights to Pennsylvania, passed to his second son John, then aged 15 years. The young Penn saw little of Stoke Poges

at this time because he was abroad. After the American Revolution in 1776 the Pennsylvania Legislature divested the Penns of their proprietorial rights leaving them only their personal lands. John Penn, with his three-quarters share of the rights, calculated that his family lost 21 million acres. The compensation voted by the Commonwealth was £130,000, and the English Parliament also voted a £4,000 annual pension in recognition of the American losses. John Penn received three quarters of each of these sums.

Returning to England in 1789, his fortune considerably enhanced, Penn set about living up to his new wealth. The Manor House was in need of considerable repair, chiefly from damp in the principal rooms. John decided to build a replacement mansion. The old Manor House was dismantled with only the west wing remaining and a new mansion built in the middle of the Park. This was a site originally suggested to Thomas Penn in 1765 by Field Marshal Sir George Howard and Capability Brown, who had been employed at nearby Stoke Place. Humphry Repton also advised on the siting.

The new building started with Nasmith as architect and was completed by James Wyatt. Wyatt also designed the sarcophagus to commemorate Thomas Gray and the Coke column. Repton was also commissioned in 1792 to improve the Park, including the bridge across the lake. His Red Book on the Stoke Park improvements has survived.

In 1802 John Penn, like his father, removed a building to improve his view. This was the old vicarage which was replaced with a Gothic-style building in Park Road, one of the few small houses designed by James Wyatt. In 1810 work was started on the garden to the west of the new mansion with southerly views towards Windsor Castle. This

Pub.ᵈ Janʸ 10ᵗʰ 1804, by Dighton, Charᵍ Croſs.

A GOOD OLD PENN,

From the wing of a GOOD OLD COCK

26 Cartoon of John Penn published in 1804. (Penn Gray Museum, South Bucks District Council.)

27 Bas-relief by John Deare representing a check received by Caesar in his invasion of Britain. (By permission of Crane Davies Limited, the Manor House, Stoke Poges.)

garden, lost in the 1860s, was based on the classical style of the poet Mason who visited Stoke in 1792 and corresponded with Penn. In 1804 Penn enlarged his new mansion, increasing the length of its library and employing a librarian to care for the books. The panels above the bookcases incorporated 12 grisailles[2] by Robert Smirke. A marble bas-relief by John Deare was also installed above a fireplace, having been commissioned from the artist in Rome together with a marble bust of Penn himself. The bas-relief, representing a check received by Caesar in his invasion of Britain, is now in the Manor House. The bust of Penn is in Eton College Library and a plaster replica is in St Giles' Church.

In 1834 John died and for the next ten years his brother Granville lived at Stoke Park but in 1844 Granville's son, called Granville John, inherited

28 Replica of a bust of John Penn by John Deare in the Penn Pew, St Giles' Church.

29 St Giles' Church at the time of the Penns showing the ancient door in the west wall. Later the lower part was bricked up and the upper portion converted into a window. This window now contains a memorial to the men who fell in the Second World War and incorporates the Bicycle Window.

the estate. An American, John Jay Smith, stayed at Stoke Park House in 1845 not long after the death of Granville. He wrote this description of life in an English country house during its heyday:

> The family at Stoke Park then [1845] consisted of the widow of Granville Penn—her husband then very recently deceased—a very old lady, Granville John (son of Granville), three unmarried sisters, and the youngest brother William, who was educated for the bar. The mother, the three daughters and the three sons are now [1867] all deceased but a more happy and united family than they formed twenty five years ago it would be difficult to describe.
>
> Their surroundings were of the very first class, as regards a truly noble residence, an extension and perfectly kept park, abounding in deer and other game, a library of great size and value, liveried servants, fine horses and coaches, with everything that could make life desirable.
>
> The picturesque park that has seen so many successive generations come and go, as we rambled amongst its beautiful and ancient trees, was as silent as any scene in our own native forests. The servants had mown the extensive lawns, the hot-house gardeners had set out the Italian portico with newly flowered plants, covering the pots with lycopodiums and mosses, and the attendants had all disappeared before breakfast was announced; every sound was stilled and the place was all one's own.
>
> The deer silently wandered amongst the ferns half as tall as themselves; the librarian, himself a learned man and an author of merit, was at his post to hand the guests any book they required.

One felt assured on passing the great entrance hall beneath a funeral hatchment of the late proprietor, that he was not entering the house of consistent Quakers, for one of the first objects was a pair of small brass cannon, taken by Admiral Penn in his Dutch wars, elegantly mounted and polished; and near by, opening on the left, was a fine billiard-room. Family prayers were not neglected; the numerous servants were regularly assembled, as is the usual custom in England; the service of the day is reverently read, and all, from the head of the house to the humblest individual, on their knees to give thanks for mercies received.

The house was not wanting in memorials to Pennsylvania, a large portion of the Treaty Tree, sent by some members of the Historical Society, with a silver label on it, ornamenting the grand drawing room of the second storey which was reached by a long, and rather fatiguing marble staircase. The birds of Pennsylvania too were represented in elegant glass cases, together with Indian relics, and a finely preserved beaver which animal was once the annual tribute of the Penns to the Crown.[3]

Granville John inherited an estate he could not afford to maintain. He moved to West End House, the former home of Thomas Gray, which he enlarged and renamed Stoke Court. Stoke Park was offered for rent and in 1848 sold to Henry Labouchere, a cabinet minister later created Baron Taunton.

Then in 1851 Granville John also sold Stoke Court and such were the financial pressures on him that in June of that year Sotheby's, in a six-day sale, disposed of the first half of the Stoke Park library assembled by John Penn.[4] The next month he also sold a large collection of paintings, including West's important picture of William Penn's treaty with the Indians, painted for Thomas Penn in 1771. A number of Thomas Gray items, including the poet's manuscripts and editions of his books with the poet's own notations, were also sold. In 1854 financial necessity again forced another sale including further and more valuable Gray manuscripts.

And so the last sane male Penn died in 1867 dragged down by financial worry. Granville John's brother, the Reverend Thomas Penn, who was insane and whose affairs were in the hands of his cousins, died two years later.

Ten

The Poor of Stoke Poges

Until 1894 the Vestry administered secular as well as church matters. It was responsible for collection of rates, upkeep of the highways, appointing parish officers and the relief of the poor. The Vestry had evolved from the 16th century onwards as a unit of local government, following the decline of the manorial and hundred courts. It was a meeting of the inhabitants of a village or the more substantial ratepayers, usually presided over by the local clergyman. The name vestry derives from the room attached to a church where vestments are kept.

Most of the Stoke Poges records have been preserved, including the Vestry minute books from 1794. They give an invaluable insight into how the parish was governed, especially how the poor were treated. People who struggled through life and managed to pay their way might only appear in the records at birth, marriage and death. If they became poor enough 'to go on the parish' they could have numerous entries.

The foundation of the poor law administration was the great Poor Law Act of Elizabeth I, passed in 1601. This, with subsequent amending Acts, lasted over two centuries. It charged the churchwardens, and from two to four substantial householders nominated as overseers of the poor, to administer poor relief. The able-bodied unemployed were to be set to work and in Stoke Poges this was in the parish gravel pits or maintaining the local roads. Those unable to work received other help.

The key to the poor law was the Law of Settlement and Removal passed in 1662. This gave the churchwardens and overseers the power to apply to the justices for a warrant to remove any newcomer to his place of birth, whether or not he needed relief, unless he rented land or property at £10 or more per annum. This law was amended in 1795 to add a provision that no person could be removed until he had actually become a charge upon the poor rate.

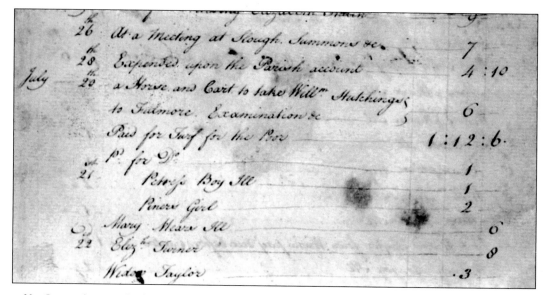

30 Overseers' account book entry 1787 recording the 6 shillings paid in 1786 for William Hutchings' examination to establish his place of birth.

31 Bill for conveying Thomas Noris and his family to his place of birth.

The first step before removal to a person's place of birth was an examination by a magistrate who established the facts and made an order. In 1786 six shillings was spent in taking William Hutchings to the nearest magistrate in Fulmer for such an examination.

Once the order was made the cost of removal could be expensive but cheaper than maintaining a family out of the rates for a long period.

The bill reveals that it cost Stoke Poges £3 7s. 6d. to convey Thomas Noris and his family to Wanborough in 1784. The journey of 65 miles took five days, an indication of how slow transport was in those days owing to the bad state of the roads. Another example of trying to safeguard the parish from a potential future expense occurred in 1795. The overseers paid £5 6s. 9d. for expenses of a wedding. The girl was pregnant and she and her child would have become a charge on the parish. The father of the child was from another parish and, if the couple married—and doubtless pressure was brought to bear—they could be sent to the legal parish of the father. It was worth £5 6s.

9d. to save a possible future expense of keeping mother and child in the workhouse for a number of years.

Stoke Poges parish records contain much detail of how money was spent to relieve poverty. The unemployed, widows, the aged and infirm, often received weekly payments. The incomes of the poorer classes left no margin to cope with emergencies and the account books show many *ad hoc* payments for sickness, medical attention, clothing, burial expenses and other sundry items. The most tragic entry perhaps is one dated 7 November 1817 which reads 'Hillier one week 4s., relieved ill 3s., funeral 7s.- total 14s.'

Whilst paupers could remain in their own homes, sometimes they were forced to go to the parish poorhouse. Until 1788 the poorhouse was quite small and judging by the small rent paid for it just a cottage. Ideally the best solution was for the poor to earn their keep and the ratepayers would have welcomed an opportunity presented to the parish by Mr. James Squib.

Eleven

The House that Squib Built

In 1771 Mr. James Squib, a lace buyer of London, proposed to establish 'a manufactory in the Parish of Stoke Poges for the spinning of sneal, weaving of hoods and other manufactorys'. Squib applied to the Manor Court of Stoke Poges and requested permission to enclose a piece of the Common near West End and Morralls End on which he could erect a house and several sheds. Although commoners enjoyed certain rights over the common, the Lord of the Manor, Thomas Penn, owned the soil and subsoil, including mineral rights. It was necessary to secure the consent of both to enclose part of the common. The Manor Court was convened, a rare event, the only other recorded occasion being in 1809 when Thomas Penn's son John was seeking to enclose the whole of Stoke Common.

The Court met on 26 September 1771 and it is recorded that it ordered that 'Mr. Slaughter the foreman and such other of the said Jurors as shall chuse or think proper not less than nine in number do meet tomorrow at the sign of the Five Bells at Morralls End aforesaid at Eight o'clock in the morning in order to set out the said spot of ground'. Having staked out the site, a lease was to be granted for 99 years, subject to the consent of Thomas Penn.

There were conditions attached to the lease. Firstly, should Squib cease to carry on a manufactory then the lease would be surrendered to the Churchwardens and Overseers of the Poor, subject to compensation not exceeding £300. Second, the poor were to be instructed in weaving, but any persons brought into the parish

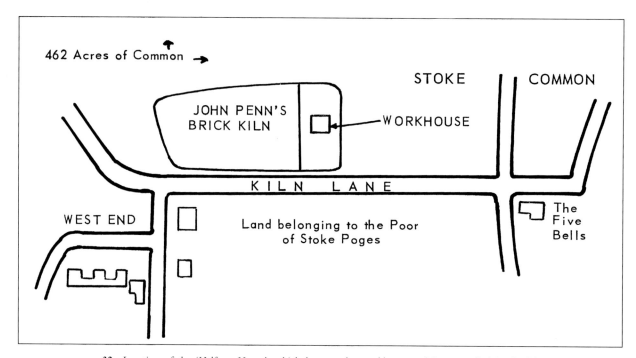

32 Location of the 'Halfway House', which became the workhouse and is now called 'Uplands'.

33 'Uplands', Rogers Lane.

to be employed in instructing the poor were to deliver to the Churchwardens and Overseers a certificate of their being legally settled elsewhere. This would certify that the individual was the responsibility of another parish which would take him back in the event of his requiring poor relief. Third, Squib was not to hire any servant by the year nor take any apprentice for any number of years without the consent of the Minister, Churchwardens and Overseers. Apprentices bound by indentures and unmarried servants hired for a year could gain a legal settlement. The last two conditions were to ensure that newcomers did not become a charge upon the poor rate of Stoke Poges.

The map shows that the area of land was about one acre located half way between West End and Morralls End, where the *Five Bells* was located. This

The Overseers of Stoke
To Elis by Saml Harman   £   s   d

1790
Apll
28   a Strong Iron bound Porfenyhim 45 Gall   18 .. 9
          3 Coolers .. 72 Gall   1 .. 10 .. —
          a hop Sive —   3 .. 6
          Tap & tap wase —   1 .. 3
          Tunill & handle Bowle — —   5 .. 6
          a Large Bowle —   3 .. 4 ..

                    By Cash - —   3 .. 4 —

                                      Ballance   0 0 0
                          S Harman

1791
May 4,   Paid Mr Buckland a Bill for Goods to the Work
          House from the Kiln to Build a Oven —
          and a place of Confinment   5 14 11½
          to a sonions for Way Silver omited   1 0
          to a Invatrey of wansal goods and Cloaths
          at the worke house omited   0 4 0
          for Warrants & Expences at Colenbrook — 14 .. 0
          paid Joseph Billington for Pontins Widow — 9 .. 0
          Do 6 paid Expences at Joseph Billingtons — 3 .. 0
          13 Delivered to Mr Ambrose Clark with the book 3 .. 9½

is the reason why the house, when it was built, was called 'The Halfway House'. The map also shows that it fronted on to Kiln Lane, so called because the Lord of the Manor's brick kiln was alongside it. The Lord of the Manor owned the right to brick earth from the Common and Kiln Lane was its southern boundary in those days. Today, the house is known as 'Uplands' and Kiln Lane is now Rogers Lane.

In 1784 Squib sold the house to Thomas Dibbs and apparently extricated himself from the obligation in the Manor Court Agreement to surrender it to the Parish. The agreement did contain a provision that if the manufactory ceased and the lease was surrendered Squib would be compensated for any buildings erected up to a value of £300. Perhaps the parish officers were unwilling to pay the compensation. Four years later, in 1788, the Overseers leased the house from Dibbs for 40 years, at a rent of £6 6s. 0d. per annum, for use as the parish workhouse. The site was described as one acre with an orchard on the north side. The Overseers' accounts for the year 1788/9 show that the total expenditure for the year on the poor was £548. This included £123 for the purchase of goods for the newly opened workhouse.

34 (top) The Overseers' accounts of 28 April 1790 for the purchase of equipment for making beer.

35 (bottom) The record of a payment to Mr. Buckland to build an oven and a place of confinement. The kiln referred to was next door to the workhouse. What was the place of confinement? Was it a gaol? There was an item the following year for two pairs of handcuffs which cost 7s. 0d.

Twelve

The Workhouse and Mrs. Parker Sedding

The workhouse presented the Vestry with continuing problems and, when expenditure increased, as it did in most years, economies were sought. Contracting out responsibility for looking after the poor for a fixed sum, called 'farming the poor', was tried in 1790. The cost was £300. In 1793 the cost was £315 and, in addition, £81 11s. 4d. was paid for clothing and £17 17s. 0d. for 'doctoring'. In 1801, when the parish population was 741, expenditure on the poor rose to £1,136 and to £1,366 the following year. Expenditure fell to £514 in 1803 because it was decided to pay the workhouse master only 3s. 6d. per inmate per week.

from 1 January 1805. For this salary he agreed 'to superintend all the poor committed to his care, to undertake the entire management of the Workhouse and to instruct the paupers (as well as those within the Workhouse as all others sent to him for the same purpose by the overseer or overseers) in the manufacture of worsteds in all its different branches'.

Mr. Lewis was no improvement on his predecessors. In 1805 Mrs. Parker Sedding, a well-to-do widow who rented and managed her own farm in the Baylis area of the parish, visited the workhouse and recorded her disgust at this 'seminary of

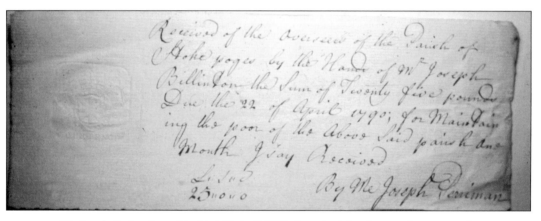

36 Joseph Perriman's receipt, dated 22 April 1790, for maintaining the poor for one month.

Despite several changes in the post of workhouse master the dissatisfaction continued. In 1804 the Vestry decided to look into the state of the workhouse. The Vestry minutes recorded that 'the workhouse appears in a very bad condition, no work is being done in it upon the wheels already provided by the Parish or in any other way'. They sacked the master, giving him three months notice to quit, and a new master, a Mr. Thomas Lewis, was appointed at a salary of £25 per annum

idleness and immorality'. 'The workhouse was filthy and devoid of every vestige of comfort and decency, old and young, men, women and little children, sick and well, the genuine unemployed and they who ever sought work in the hope of never finding it, were—at least during the day time—herded promiscuously together'.

The next year, 1806, Mrs. Sedding was appointed Overseer of the Poor. She promptly moved into the workhouse and spent a month

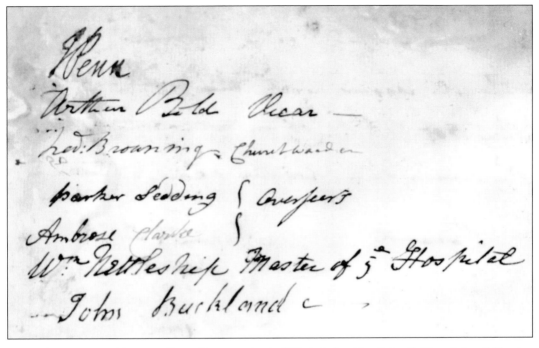

37   The signatures of those attending a Vestry meeting in 1806, including Mrs. Parker Sedding, Arthur Bold and John Penn.

there, setting the poor to work, fumigating the clothing and bedding at a time when the process was barely known, providing wholesome food and instruction in simple employments. The children were lodged apart and instructed in reading and spinning. A visitor wrote enthusiastically 'of one little boy in petticoats engaged at spinning earned 2d. per day and had it all to himself, and as he knew he was to be put in boys cloaths when he earned them, he was working very diligently indeed to obtain them'.

The Vestry met 'to take into consideration amongst other matters, the report of the Overseer as to the circumstances in the conduct of the Master of the Workhouse which appear to require some explanations'. The efficient Mrs. Parker Sedding also reported that some improper charges had been made for butter, tea and beer. The Vestry resolved 'that henceforth the allowances for ale to the Master be limited to eight pints per week, that no fresh butter be used in the Workhouse at the Parish expense and that the sum of one shilling and six-pence be the whole allowance for tea and sugar'. In that same year the magistrates of the Hundred of Stoke, meeting at Salt Hill, put on record their appreciation of the vigorous administration of Mrs. Parker Sedding. The magistrates were required to approve vestry accounts.

In 1812 Mrs. Sedding gave £200 'for the benefit of the Parish in all succeeding times in gratitude to God Almighty for the blessings she had received in Stoke'. This sum was to purchase £333 6s. 8d. of annuities to be placed in Trust, the dividends to be used one half towards the support of the School or of a Sunday or other School for the instruction of the children of the poor people of the Parish, and the other half to buy bread for the poor widows of the Parish. This investment still forms part of the Stoke United Charities.

Thirteen
The Workhouse Rules

In January 1826 the Vestry Committee resolved that 'John Hedge who has falsely misrepresented himself to be a proper object for the Workhouse should be turned out'. The decision followed a letter from Lord Montague of Ditton. Ditton was then, although detached, part of the parish of Stoke Poges. Hedge had said that he had long been out of work but Lord Montague wrote, 'he had at that time been employed in my service for six weeks at ten shillings a week. I understand that on his way to the workhouse he stopped at a public house and spent money on drink which I can easily believe as he has long been known in this part of the Parish as a notoriously idle drunkard and in my opinion is a very unfit inmate of a workhouse'.

During his brief stay in the workhouse John Hedge would have been required to obey the workhouse rules which were introduced in the previous year, August 1825.

38 Part of the document listing the workhouse rules.

RULES and REGULATIONS TO BE OBEID IN THE POOR HOUSE OF STOKE POGES

1st No person will be allowed to deviate from any lawful command given by the governor or governess. Every person to attend divine service on Sundays mornings and afternoons, anyone neglecting the same without the governor's leave loses one hot dinner.

2nd The governor to read prayers Tuesday and Friday evenings every person able to attend.

3rd The children be taught their catechism once a week or oftener if necessary and to read lessons from the testaments as often as convenient and to say grace before and after meales.

4th The governor or governess always to carve for the poor and see they sit down decently and in good order.

5th The poor to be summoned for their meales as follows. Breckfast at eight in summer and nine in winter, dinner always at one o'clock, supper at eight in summer, and seven in winter, one hour allowed at dinner, and half an hour at breckfast, the meales always to be eaten in the hall and no one leaves the room till the meale is finished.

6th The working people to get them some refreshment before they go to work if found necessary.

7th The governor of the house shall employ any of the poor he may think proper, to work in the garden, clean the house, dress victuals, bake or brew or .... about the house .... from six in the morning until seven at night and from eight in the morning till seven at night in winter.

8th Any person refusing to worke shall be fed on bread and water for dinner, one, two or three times and otherwise punished at the discretion of the parish officers.

9th The governor is particularly requested to take care that no Spirituous liqours be brought into the house, any person found drunk, swearing, quarreling, fighting or any way disturbing the peace of the house shall be confined and dealt with accordingly.

10th No person to be admitted into the house without an order from one of the officers nor any person permitted to go off the premises without the governor or governess leave and such persons not returning in good order at the time appointed are not to go again for one month, and if any one be found begging to lose the next hot meal.

11th The poor employed out of the house to worke the same hours as the other labourers employed with them, every man, woman, and child shall receive two pence out of every shilling as encouragement money, no person will be allowed to take their earnings, but the governor, and he will place the same to the credit of the parish, in his monthly accounts.

12th The governor to see that the sick and lame be duly attended to by the surgeon and that they follow his directions, the governess to see that the children are kept clean by washing, combing etc. etc. and to cause all beds to be made, the rooms passages and all other useful parts of the house swept every day, after breckfast, and washed once a week and oftener if found necessary, the chamber utensils never to be emptied out of the windows any person so doing will be punished accordingly.

13th The chamber utensils to be brought down every morning before breckfast the bed room windows to be kept open at all times during the day when the weather permits.

14th The governor or governess to see all persons in the house go to bed by nine o'clock in the summer and at eight in the winter and to see all fires and candles properly put out.

15th Any person belonging to the house found guilty of stealing, selling their provisions or clothing, or other breach of trust, shall be punished to the utmost severity of the law.

16th These rules to be read every Sunday after dinner, no persons leave the room until they are read.

17th The governor is particularly requested to see all the foregoing rules are duly attended to.

AUGUST 1825

Church Wardens   Overseers

Note: the missing words in the 7th rule have been gnawed from the original document by the church mice.

Fourteen

Mr. Robarts the Surgeon

Medical treatment for the poor was arranged by the overseers. It was not always administered by a surgeon, hence this entry dated 4 October 1788 'for John Buckland for bleedin Tom Turner 3 times 1s. 6d.'. John Buckland was the village blacksmith. Unfortunately he was not successful with this particular form of treatment and two days later is another entry—'for laying out Thomas Turner & Flannel & Bread & Cheese & Beer & Minester & Clark & Afterdavid 15s. 4d.'. It was the custom to supply the bearers with refreshment at a funeral.

From 1831 to 1835 the parish contracted with Mr. Robarts, a surgeon of Burnham, to provide medical treatment for the poor. He was, however, twice found guilty of neglect. In 1831 Mr. Nickson, the vicar, laid before the Vestry two documents complaining of non-attendance of the parochial surgeon to the sick. It was decided to send the complaints to Robarts to enable him to 'rebut the charge which is alleged against him'. In addition, because Robarts had complained to the vicar of the inadequacy of his salary, he was requested to

state what he thought would be an adequate salary. A fortnight later the Vestry minutes record receipt of the following tender:

> To attend the Poor of Stoke Poges and casualties therein, including those paupers resident in Langley, Upton, Wexham and Farnham, with all fractures and operations, coroners' inquests, vaccinations and cases of midwifery requiring more than common assistance if such shall occur, excluding recent sexual disorders of course. Trusses to be supplied at 12s., extra doubles, or lower if can obtain them. If the Vestry would prefer £45 to include all charges Oakley Green included I would not object. Signed Robarts.

Paupers in other parishes who were born in Stoke Poges remained the responsibility of Stoke Poges, hence the reference to neighbouring parishes. The Vestry accepted this increased annual charge but only on condition that the surgeon paid more attention to the sick poor of the parish and that his contract be reviewed every six months.

There is little information as to the treatments prescribed for the sick. It is recorded that in

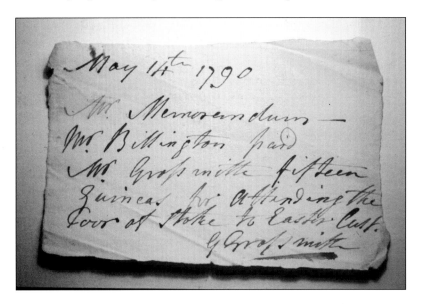

39 Mr. Grossmith the surgeon's receipt, dated 14 May 1790, for attending to the poor for one year.

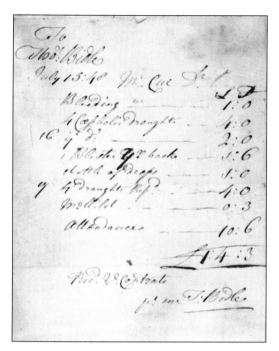

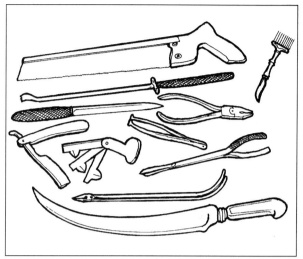

40 A surgeon's bill for medical attention, dated 15 July 1748, an earlier period than that of Mr. Robarts. The first recorded parish payment for a doctor was 9s. 0d. to a surgeon for Judith West in 1657.

41 Typical surgical instruments of the period.

September 1831 eight shillings was paid to Edward Hughes for his expenses in being brought back from the Middlesex Hospital. The doctor at that hospital having recommended that Hughes' case was one for which the Bath waters would be serviceable, it was agreed 'to remove him there forthwith, that the expenses of his conveyance be defrayed, and that a deposit of £3 be allowed'. It seems that Robarts performed operations in the workhouse for when these were required patients were admitted to the workhouse.

The following year, 1832, Mr. Robarts' annual contract was renewed and his salary paid half yearly. However, in January 1833 the Vestry minutes record another serious complaint. 'It appearing to the Select Vestry that John Ware's child was grievously burnt at about eight o'clock in the morning of Wednesday 23rd January, that a messenger was sent to Burnham who informed Mr. Robarts' assistant of it at eleven o'clock on the same day, and

the father of the child saw Mr. Robarts himself at six the same evening, and yet neither Mr. Robarts nor his assistant visited the child until the following night, Thursday, between 5 and 6 o'clock, the Overseers were requested to speak to Mr. Robarts on the subject.' Mr. Robarts appeared before the next meeting to explain his late attendance and it was decided that 'what he said in extenuation did not entirely absolve him from charge of neglect, and it was ordered that this resolution be communicated to Mr. Robarts'.

However, three years later national legislation abolished local control. Centralised administration led to 'Union' workhouses covering groups of parishes. Stoke Poges, when it protested, was accused of mismanagement of its workhouse and Mr. Robarts testified as to the high standards maintained in Stoke Poges, but sadly it became part of the Eton Union.

Fifteen
The Enclosure Controversy

In 1806, when John Penn first contemplated his Enclosure Bill for Stoke Poges and Wexham, Stoke Common was much larger than it is today. Penn wanted to enclose the whole of the Common but others were concerned that the loss of common rights would gravely disadvantage the poor. The intervention of a small group of the local gentry saved part of the Common.

Penn was the main instigator of the enclosure plan. He would gain land in lieu of his manorial rights to soil and to dig brick earth from the Common. There was already a brick kiln on the edge of the Common in Rogers Lane, then known as Kiln Lane. The site opposite the present school,

42 John Penn.

where the brick earth was dug out, is now below road level.

There was a right of turbary which meant that the peat-based turves were cut in late summer, burnt off and stored for winter use. Coal was expensive until the coming of the railways in the 1840s made transporting it much cheaper. There was also a grazing right on the Common. Penn proposed that a sum of £50 should be distributed to the poor as compensation for their loss of common rights. Between 60 and 80 families depended on the Common for fuel and grazing.

The enclosure proposals would be of major benefit to the southern part of the Parish. Here much of the land was still divided into strips, a relic of the medieval field system. In medieval times the large open fields were parcelled out in long narrow unfenced strips and farmed in common, using the two- or three-field system of rotating crops. Each owner's strips were scattered to secure a fair distribution of good and indifferent land. Over the centuries piecemeal enclosure and some consolidation had taken place and gradually changed the landscape. By 1802, as the sketch map illustrates, there were fewer owners but holdings were scattered, making them unsuitable for efficient farming. Enclosure and land exchanges would create larger fields of between 10 and 20 acres. Drainage would be easier and fencing less costly. Provision would be made for new and improved road construction. Farming would be more profitable because the new agricultural machinery could be used. Tithes could also be extinguished by the allotment of land in lieu.

The first notification of John Penn's plans was in August 1806 when some of the freeholders were told of his intention to apply to Parliament

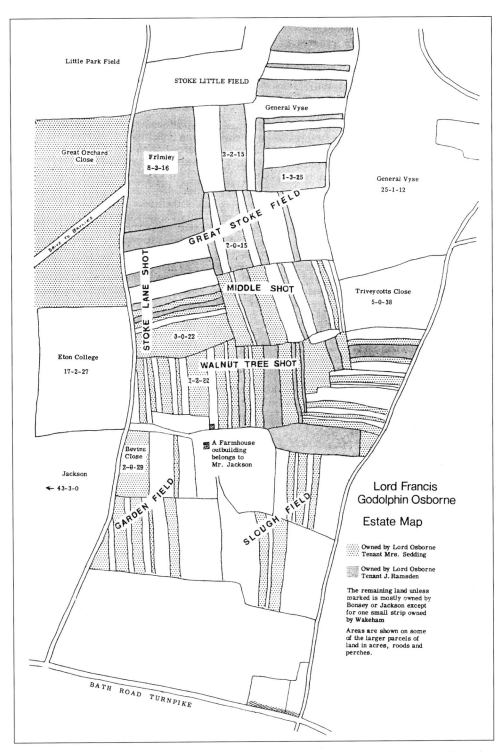

43 Lord Francis Godolphin Osborne's estate map of 1802. Lord Francis owned 484 acres out of a total of 2,835 in Stoke Poges. This section of his estate map shows the open fields divided into strips.

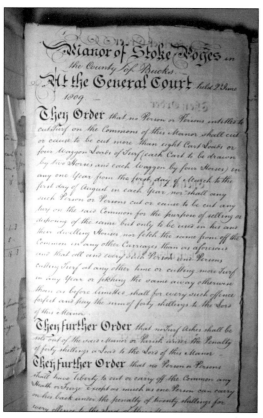

44 The record of the manorial court held on 2 June 1809.

for leave to promote a private enclosure Bill. This prompted two local clergymen, William Nettleship, Master of the Hastings Hospital, and William George Freeman, a retired minister and Justice of the Peace, to write letters addressed to the resident gentry of the Parish.[1]

They asked for resistance to this measure which they felt was harsh and oppressive to the labouring poor. The proposed plan would 'rob' the cottagers and their families, upwards of 370 persons, of their invaluable privileges of common. The letter urged 'a strenuous decided opposition' to the projected enclosure. In another letter William Nettleship set out the difference in fuel costs between turf from the Common and coal which was expensive to transport. Just under two tons of coal cost

£4 16s. 3d. as against 16s. for the expense of cutting and drying turf.

Two years elapsed before Penn again promoted enclosure. In 1808 he wrote to the Reverend Arthur Bold, Vicar of Stoke Poges, and to Bold's patron, Lord Francis Godolphin Osborne. Lord Francis was a large landowner in the Parish and in Wexham. This provoked Freeman into writing another letter to proprietors of land urging opposition. He wrote, 'We only know of three persons favourable to this robbery, Mr. Penn, Mr. Bonsey and Lord Francis Osborne; we have reason to believe his Lordship may be induced to alter his opinion.'

At this point Captain Richard William Howard Howard-Vyse, then 25 years of age and M.P. for Beverley, joined the opposition. He pressed the vicar to do his duty to the poor; perhaps he could recommend leaving out the Common. Howard-Vyse wrote that he would see Lord Montague, who owned Ditton Park, then part of the ancient parish, and would also again talk to Mr. Penn, 'tho', he added, 'I have too often and too plainly told him my mind on the subject to hope for success'. Howard-Vyse's concluding paragraph reveals his genuine concern for the poor when he writes:

> The warm interest I take in opposing this harsh measure is the only excuse I can offer for the length and urgency of this letter, which however I cannot conclude, without seriously lamenting the consequences that may follow any delicacy or reserve on your part, in making that explanation and remonstrance on the subject, which your sentiments and station make so peculiarly proper and effectual; and if the alteration I propose can be arranged, I trust the preservation of a supply of fuel so essential to the comfort of so many families, will not be an ungrateful recompense for any trouble you may be kind enough to take in this business.

This led to letters from Bold to Penn, to his superior the Bishop of Lincoln and to Lord Francis, all seeking to safeguard the interests of the poor. There are in all 13 letters preserved in the parish records recording this controversy.

The following year, 1809, Penn's agent Robert Cole convened a meeting of the Manorial Court. The Court to our knowledge had not met since 1771. The object may have been to set out formally for the purpose of the Bill the rights existing on Stoke Common. The record of the proceedings sets out in detail the rights of turbary and grazing. Grazing was related to the size of land ownership.

The last enclosure letter was written by Arthur Bold on 24 March 1810 and in it he referred to the clause in the Bill, given its first reading on 14 March 1810, under which an allotment of 200 acres was to be made to the poor. This was evidently the compromise that opposition to the measure had secured. The 200 acres, later reduced to 196 when four acres were sold off in 1867, was used by the poor to continue the practice of cutting turves for fuel. Later in the century railways reduced transportation costs and eventually the Charity became a coal club subsidising the cost of coal.

Very few fuel allotments were made under private enclosure Acts of Parliament and the Stoke Poges allotment is by far the largest of these. The Stoke Poges and Wexham Act was passed in 1810 but not fully implemented until the Commissioners appointed under it made their Deed of Award signed and sealed on 30 January 1822. Common rights, however, had been extinguished in 1813.

Under the provisions of the Act trustees were appointed for the Poor's Fuel Allotment and they were Penn, as Lord of the Manor, the Vicar, and the Churchwardens and Overseers of the Poor. They drew up a set of rules governing the quantity of turves that could be taken in one year and laid down a defined season for cutting, from 1 May to 28 September. There were other rules including one prohibiting the selling of turf to anyone at all. Three inspectors were appointed to check the loads of turves cut, for each of which they were paid 3d. The inspectors could cut turves for those who were unable or unwilling to cut their own. They were allowed to charge 5s. per 100 turves for this service.

The consequences of enclosure for Stoke Poges when implemented in 1822 were significant. The area in the south of the Parish, some 215 acres, was reallocated into compact fields. After setting aside the 200 acres for the poor, the remaining 260 acres of the Common were divided among 53 individuals, the largest share of 80 acres being allotted to Lord Francis Godolphin Osborne. A further 973 acres of the old enclosures, half the remaining land, were also reallocated. Much of the land was subject to numerous exchanges between owners to achieve more compact holdings.

The land north of Rogers Lane, formerly part of the Common, could not have been developed in the next century but for the Enclosure Act. The Village Hall would not have been built where it is if the site had not been allotted to the Church in lieu of tithes. Bells Hill would not have been developed as a shopping centre but for a series of plots allocated in lieu of common rights and later developed as small shops and public houses. The site of the school in School Lane, built in 1876, in what until then was called Hazell Lane, was land allotted to the old Charity School.

> *Notice is hereby given,*
> **That all Persons trespassing on *Stoke Common*, by turning Cattle, Hogs, Pigs, Geese, or Ducks thereon, or in any other manner, will have them pounded, and be prosecuted according to Law; all Rights of Common having been extinguished the 7th. of *February* last, by Order of the**
> **Commissioners of the Inclosure.**
> Dated the 21st Day of *June*, 1813.

45 This notice, published in 1813, told villagers that their rights of common had been extinguished as a result of the Enclosure Act.

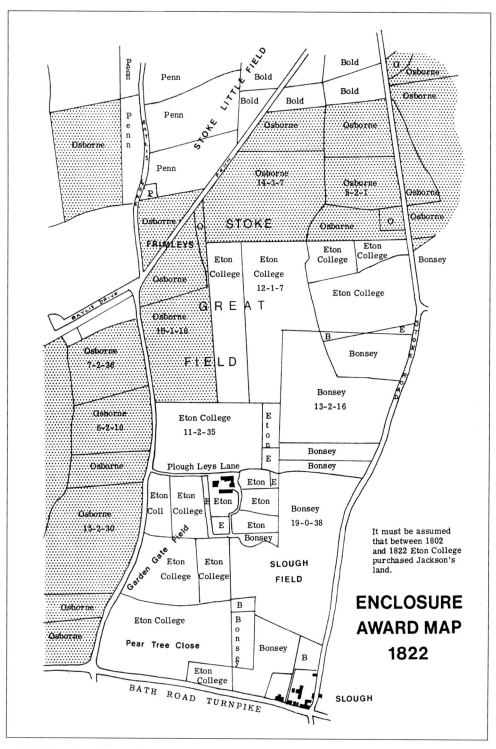

46 This section of the Enclosure Award map shows how the open fields, previously divided into strips as shown on the Godolphin Osborne estate map, were reallocated.

Lastly, what is now the B416 cutting Stoke Common in two was one of the 10 public roads defined in the Enclosure Award. The document read, 'one other public carriage or highway of the breadth of forty feet leading from Morrells End in a northward direction in its present track across Stoke Common until it enters the road between the parishes of Fulmer and Hedgerely leading to Gerrards Cross'. The area where the Village Hall now stands was know as Morrells End at that time.

Stoke Common, because it is now a rare heathland habitat, was designated as a Site of Special Scientific Interest in 1972. Its upkeep proved to be too great a demand on the limited resources of the Poor's Fuel Allotment Charity.[2] The Common was sold to South Bucks District Council in 1990. The Charity Commission then issued a new scheme and the old Poor's Fuel Allotment Charity became

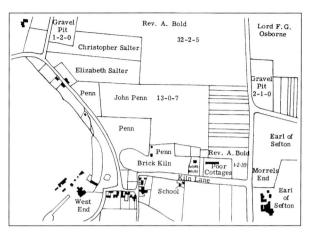

47 Part of the Enclosure Award map of 1822.

a Relief In Need Charity, with a greatly enhanced income from the investment of the proceeds of the sale.

48 The Easter Hunt with the Royal Stag Hounds—the Meet at Stoke Common, 1845.

Sixteen
Sidney Godolphin Osborne and the Poor Law Petitions

Arthur Bold died in 1831 at the age of 58 and the register entry read, 'The ever lamented Vicar of this Parish'. He had served for 28 years. Early in his incumbency he had been forced to move from the old vicarage near St Giles' Church, demolished by Penn because it spoilt his view, to a new vicarage in Park Road. He had also borne the brunt of the enclosure controversy.

He was succeeded by the Honourable and Reverend Sidney Godolphin Osborne, the third son of Lord Francis Godolphin Osborne, the patron of the living of Stoke Poges. Sidney was born in 1808 at the time of the enclosure dispute when his father had agreed to the compromise of retaining 200 acres of the common for the poor. His father's decision that he was to enter the Church was communicated to young Sidney when they were

out shooting. It is said that he accepted the decision 'without repining, but without enthusiasm'. In due course he graduated from Oxford, took Holy Orders and, in 1831, when he was 23 years of age, he became curate at Stoke Poges. The following year, the living being in the gift of his father, he became vicar.

It was only after he moved to Durweston in Dorsetshire in 1841 that Osborne achieved a national reputation as a somewhat militant philanthropist. He took a special interest in the lot of the agricultural labourer with his advocacy of better homes, higher wages and more humane treatment. He published social tracts and achieved national fame as a result of his 'lay sermons' published over a period of almost half a century in *The Times*. In 1859, when his brother succeeded to the Dukedom of Leeds, he was given the courtesy rank of a duke's son and was then known as Lord Sidney Godolphin Osborne.

In Stoke Poges, Osborne, whose initials his subsequent parishioners said stood for 'Sincere Good Outspoken', probably stamped his forceful personality on the parish. He was a striking preacher.

> His style was vigorous and incisive: his language plain, direct, and earnest. With infinite forebearance towards the sinner, especially the poor sinner, in his sermons he lashed vice and cruelty with whips of scorn … and he always dwelt fully on the practical application to daily life of the doctrine he taught. On words, phrases, sentiments, and ideals, unaccompanied by the living eloquence of a noble life, he looked down with contempt. For he himself translated into practice the doctrine he taught others.[1]

On one occasion, in what his sexton called 'highly privileged' Stoke Poges, where there was what S.G.O. called a 'deal of carriage company', a sermon on the proper religious training of children

49 Sidney Godolphin Osborne in later life.

50 The former Stoke Poges vicarage, by James Wyatt, 1802-4.

earned him a rebuke from a lady of high rank that he 'should have pointedly preached at them'.[2]

In 1834 Sidney married Emily Grenfell, the daughter of Pascoe Grenfell of Taplow Court. In 1835 the first of their four children was born and two of the others were also born in Stoke Poges. It was after the family moved that he became brother-in-law to two famous Victorians: Emily's sister Fanny married the novelist Charles Kingsley in 1844, and her other sister Charlotte married the historian J.A. Froude in 1849.

Sidney not only stamped his personality on the parish of Stoke Poges, he began writing his many tracts and pamphlets. *The Savings Bank* (1835); *The Nature of an Oath, with a few words of advice to a person, about to give evidence, etc.,* (1840) and *A word or two about the New Poor Law* (1835) were written in Stoke Poges. The last two pamphlets must have

resulted from the experience he gained in the campaign in February and March 1835 to prevent a union of parishes under the provisions of the Poor Law Amendment Act of 1834.

The object of a Union was to reduce the rate burden and a reaction against it on the grounds that the paupers would be treated less humanely was in itself unusual. Although there is no documentary evidence concerning the part played by Godolphin Osborne, apart from his signature to petitions, he was chairman of the Vestry Committee from which the village leadership came. The vicar's would have been the most influential voice.

While parishes had the duty of caring for their own poor, the results were differing standards and inequalities in the burden between one parish and another. In the main, the aged, the sick and the orphaned were taken care of in the parish workhouse. The able-bodied received outdoor relief. The new Act sought to make relief so distasteful to the poor that it would discourage its use except as a last resort. If outdoor relief could be abolished, and the workhouse regime made unpleasant, this objective would be achieved. Henceforth, the administration would be centralised in the hands of three Poor Law Commissioners who were empowered to make regulations, including the power to group parishes into 'Unions', each served by a central workhouse. Boards of Guardians would be elected by the ratepayers in the areas covered by each Union.

The Poor Law Commissioners wasted little time in implementing the new Act. On 31 January 1835 Mr. W.J. Gilbert, an assistant commissioner, held a meeting at the *Windmill Hotel* in Slough, to explain a scheme for the union of parishes in South Buckinghamshire to one hundred landowners, clergymen, churchwardens and overseers. The poor rate of all the parishes was upward of £20,000 a year and the number of paupers was 3,400. Under the new management there would be a saving of half. The centre of the new Union would be Gerrards Cross or Stoke Poges and the new scheme would come into operation on 25 March 1835.

The Stoke Poges paupers were treated benevolently, the workhouse having only 19 inmates, the remaining 99 paupers being in receipt of outdoor relief. The prospect of losing local control was viewed with displeasure. Other parishes may have accepted the Union but Stoke Poges was opposed to it. Two petitions were organised, one from the resident nobility, clergy, gentry, farmers and other rateable inhabitants to both Houses of Parliament, and the other from inhabitants, labourers and others to the House of Commons. The petition was presented to the House of Lords on 17 March 1835 by the Duke of Buckingham. It was challenged by Lord Brougham (Henry Brougham, 1778-1868, created Baron Brougham and Vaux in 1830, distinguished

lawyer and Whig politician), who claimed that the cost of poor relief was much more expensive in Stoke Poges than in all the other parishes except one in the proposed Union. The cost in Stoke Poges was 4s. 1½d. per head per week compared with between 2s. 6d. and 3s. 4d. in the others. Furthermore, the poorhouse of Stoke Poges was neglected and mismanaged. In a further exchange on 24 March Lord Brougham repeated his allegations.

As a result of these exchanges Stoke Poges published a pamphlet entitled 'Observations and Documents Respecting The Petitions Presented to Parliament from the Parish of Stoke Poges' (James Fraser, Regent Street, London, 1835). The pamphlet contained observations which answered the claims made by Lord Brougham and various documents. The first document was a Memorial sent to the Poor Law Commissioners signed by a number of residents including Godolphin Osborne. Six affidavits were included, four of which asserted that the meeting at the *Windmill Hotel* was not unanimous in its acceptance of the proposed Union and refuted the claim that their workhouse was mismanaged. The reply from the Poor Law Commissioners was also included.

The pamphlet 'Observations and Documents' contained the substance of the local case. The petitioners objected to the union with 18 other parishes. They wished to retain local control because their workhouse was well conducted but they were willing, with additions and alterations to the building, to carry out the principle of classification (segregation of men, women and children) if Stoke Poges were excluded from the union. They wished to manage their own poor-house, under direction of the Board, according to the Act. They complained that the new proposal would separate men from their families, and by this they must have meant that out relief would be abolished. The petitioners emphasised the benefits of local control.

The pauper was relieved by those 'who knew his situation' and 'he remains with his family, and in his house, till circumstances enable him to do without relief'. Under the proposed system the pauper would be sent to a central workhouse and his family broken up. They asked how the landlord would recover his rent except by distress upon the pauper's property. Four of the affidavits were from people who attended the initial meeting at the *Windmill Hotel* and these stated that the meeting had been poorly attended and not unanimous.[3] One of the three said there had been no regular notice convening the meeting and that he had heard of it accidentally. At the meeting Mr. Gilbert, the Assistant Commissioner, had explained that there would be a central poor-house on Stoke Common or Gerrards Cross Common for the able bodied. The other poor-houses would be wards of this central house in which the various classifications would be housed, the women in some, children in others and the aged and infirm also segregated. Despite the opposition, Mr. Gilbert said when closing the meeting, 'Now, gentlemen, I shall write to the Board tomorrow and say that you are unanimously agreed.' He then dissolved the meeting.

The other three affidavits refuted Lord Brougham's allegations regarding the mismanagement of the workhouse at Stoke Poges. The Assistant Commissioner had visited the workhouse and alleged that, at the time of his visit, there were three bastard children living there with 19 other individuals. The children were dirty and neglected and one of them did not know his alphabet. All this was untrue. At the time there were only 19 individuals in the poor-house *including* two bastard children. Further, the boy in question attended Sunday School regularly and could say his Catechism. As to the charge that the boys were dirty, they were only 'accidently dirty at that time from having been employed in sifting turf for the use of the workhouse'. Far from there being 19 diseased individuals there was 'not one sick individual excepting one person infirm from age and consequent debility'. One of the affidavits was from Robarts, the surgeon, and he certified that 'the workhouse had at all periods been kept in a very high standard of cleanliness, the bedding was attended to and only six paupers had been ill in January 1835 and December 1834, these from temporary illness'.

In an effort to prove a case for local control, it was pointed out that the cost of maintaining the paupers was only 2s. 10d. per head per week. Furthermore, the accounts were in order for at the close of the year every bill had been paid 'excepting the lawyer's which could not be got in'. In addition, the clergy had established such beneficial institutions as loan clubs, coal clubs and savings banks and in the summer the poor contributed to these from their wages in order to support their families in winter. As a final argument, it was stated that 'the poor were upon the whole, orderly and well conducted, and attached to the rich and their homes'.

The Poor Law Commissioners dealt with all these criticisms in a letter to the Home Secretary dated 17 March 1835. Their first proposal had been to unite 29 parishes but, after receiving petitions, they reconsidered it, and decided to divide this union into two parts. They did not consider it necessary to build a workhouse on Stoke Common and the Stoke Poges paupers would not be 'mixed with others of more distant parishes'. Familiar arguments were advanced in favour of centralisation. It would be more costly and less efficient to reduce further their compromise union, the boundaries of which were natural and convenient. Stoke Poges was in the centre of this area and could not be excluded. The financial aspects were presented

51   The Eton Union Workhouse, built in Slough in 1835 to serve the 19 parishes of South Buckinghamshire including Stoke Poges. The figures in the photograph, taken *c.*1880, are C.P. Barrett, clerk to the Board of Guardians, and W.P. Phillips, the workhouse master.

in a somewhat different light to the claims of the petitioners. The Parish was not as highly rated as others but it could not be excluded on these grounds since in the new arrangement Stoke would only contribute for its own paupers. The expenditure on the poor of Stoke was 'somewhat diminished by extensive charities and the benevolent disposition of many of its inhabitants' but support of the poor was still a heavy burden.

Despite the petitions and the pamphlet, a final order establishing the new union was issued to the

overseers to operate from 25 March 1835 and, later that year, work commenced on building a central workhouse in Slough. This building, standing in 12 acres, built to accommodate 440 persons at a cost of £4,559, still exists and is known today as Upton Hospital.

Seventeen

Stoke Park 1848-1908

The Right Honourable Henry Labouchere purchased Stoke Park in 1848. Henry's father Peter César was a senior partner in the banking and merchant house Hope of Amsterdam. Both he and his son married Barings. Henry, who was born in 1798, was elected to the House of Commons at the early age of 28 as a Whig in a by-election. In 1830 he was returned for the borough of Taunton and continued to represent it until 1859 when he was created Baron Taunton.

Henry held various cabinet posts during his political career, including President of the Board of Trade in 1839 and again in 1847, and Secretary of State for the Colonies in 1855. He was a highly respected man and a hard working administrator. He was described by Lord Campbell as 'a very pretty speaker' and 'such a perfect gentleman that in the House of Commons he is heard with peculiar favour'. He served as one of the commissioners for the Great Exhibition of 1851 and presided over two government commissions.

Both Henry and his father were notable patrons of the arts. Both acquired works by Thorwaldsen, the Danish sculptor, and five reliefs in plaster by the artist were let into the walls of what is now the hall of Stoke Park Mansion. A sixth work, 'The Ages of Love', was transferred to the Penn Gray Museum in Church Cottage in 1929 and donated to the Danish Embassy in London in 1962 by the Mobbs Memorial Trust. The Danish sculptor lived and worked in Rome where Henry met him for the first time in 1836. Thorwaldsen included his own portrait and that of Henry Labouchere in his plaster relief 'Homer Reciting', a work now in the Thorwaldsen Museum in Copenhagen.[1]

Henry's art collection included an unfinished painting which Gustav Waagen attributed to Michelangelo when he saw the collection being moved into Stoke Park Mansion in 1850. Later it became known as the 'Manchester Madonna' and is now in the National Gallery.[2] After being created Baron Taunton, Henry transferred his moveable collection in 1858 to a house he had built near Bridgwater in Somerset. Meanwhile he let Stoke Park until he sold it in 1863 to Edward Coleman. During Taunton's ownership of Stoke Park Sir Edwin Landseer painted many pictures of the deer in the park, including the 'Monarch of the Glen' in 1851. Lord Taunton died in 1869 and, since he had three daughters and no sons, the barony became extinct.

Edward Coleman (1834–85), who was the next owner of Stoke Park, was a wealthy young stockbroker. He lived in princely style and as well as Stoke Park, and the nearby Duffield Estate where his parents lived, he also owned a London town house in Grosvenor Square. A staunch Conservative, he was a friend of Disraeli who supported his application to become a member of the Carlton Club in 1866. He was active locally as a magistrate and, when the local School Board was formed in 1874, he became the chairman. This Board was responsible for building the new school in School Lane in 1876. In 1879 he was High Sheriff of Buckinghamshire. During his ownership he became a patron of Landseer, who continued to be a regular visitor, using the stags as models. Coleman improved the red deer stock in the park. From the time of Charles II deer were kept for specialised breeding and parks became deer farms rather than hunting grounds. Both William III and George III imported German red deer and some of George III's imports were presented to John Penn in 1781. However, Stoke Park's deer were at their best during Coleman's ownership and he introduced specialised

52 Henry Labouchere, Lord Taunton, by W.M. Tweedie, *c.*1850. (By permission of the National Portrait Gallery.)

53 'The Ages of Love' by Bertell Thorwaldsen, Queen Mary's interpretation of which, when she visited the Penn-Gray Museum in 1930, was: 'It is the dream of life'.

54 Mr. and Mrs. Wilberforce Bryant at Stoke Park Mansion in 1892. (The Wilder Collection.)

feeding to improve the herd, especially the antler growth.

Coleman had financial problems because of enormous losses of some £200,000 and a depression in the coal trade from which he derived a large part of his income. In 1881 three of Landseer's paintings he had commissioned made large sums at auction. 'Man Proposes, God Disposes' (1864) was sold to Thomas Holloway for £6,615 and now hangs in Royal Holloway College. This painting was an epitaph for the Victorian explorer Sir John Franklin whose party disappeared in the Arctic in 1847 and whose remains were found 12 months later. The other two paintings—'The Chase (or Stag Pursued by a Greyhound)' (1866) and 'Well-Bred Sitters who never say they are bored'—were sold for £5,250 each. Unfortunately, Coleman became bankrupt in 1883 and his property was administered by a trustee and committee. Stoke

Park was sold eventually to Wilberforce Bryant for £75,000 in 1887, two years after Coleman's death.

The son of William Bryant, the founder of Bryant and May, Wilberforce continued the deer herd and exported some of his stock to New Zealand.[3] A magistrate and Deputy Lieutenant of the County, he was High Sheriff in 1892. After Bryant died in 1906, the mansion was empty for two years until the estate of some 500 acres was acquired by 'Pa' Lane Jackson (who founded the Corinthian Sporting Club in 1884). He formed the Stoke Poges Land Company Limited and leased the Mansion and half of the land, some 250 acres, to the Stoke Poges Golf Club for a period of 50 years. He sold the other half for development. And so the great days of the deer park came to an end with the animals being sent to other parks and to forests in the Scottish Highlands.

Eighteen
Stoke Park—The Golf Club

In 1908 Nick Lane Jackson, or 'Pa' as he was known, set about converting the Stoke Park Mansion into a country club. The main sports offered to members would be tennis, cricket and golf. The great golf course designer Harry Shapland Colt landscaped the 27-hole course. He was the greatest authority at that time on golf-course architecture. Membership was limited and subscriptions were fixed at £10 10s. for gentlemen and £5 5s. for ladies. In addition to the excellent and spacious club rooms in the Mansion, the prospectus stated there would also be upwards of forty bedrooms and sitting rooms for the benefit of members who wished to reside at the Club. The president was H.H. Prince Albert of Schleswig-Holstein, the vice president was Earl Howe. Four distinguished local residents, Lord Decies, Henry

Allhusen, H. Howard-Vyse and E.H. Parry, joined a committee of 11 which included the Earl of Chesterfield and the Earl of Kinnoul.

The remaining land which stretched eastwards was sold for development. It included Fir Tree Avenue, Church Lane to its junction with the B416, as well as the land in Park Road and Stoke Poges Lane now the perimeter of the golf course. Individually designed houses were built to retain the character of the park. The Stoke Poges Estate Company's brochure quoted the easy access to places such as Ascot and Hawthorne Hill Racecourses, and that Harrods and other select stores delivered by motor van every day.

The Great Western Railway Company ran services of motor omnibuses, one going by Salt Hill and the other by Stoke Green to Farnham Royal.

GOLF CLUB ENTRANCE. STOKE POGES.

55   The entrance from Church Lane with the two lodges, built *c*.1800, probably by Wyatt.

56   The Mansion and Repton's bridge seen from the lake.

There was a motor service between Slough and Stoke Poges Club serving the residents of the estate nearby. The brochure also included a timetable of trains between Slough and Paddington indicating that the estate was designed for those who wanted a quick (25 minutes) link with London for business, but could still live in the country. Thus the 'commuters' arrived, although on a small scale.

Within two or three years Stoke Park was generally considered to be the best inland course in the country. Many members of the Royal family played on the course including King Edward VII. By 1912 membership reached the limit of 900 with a waiting list of a further 200. The Club's president, Prince Albert, was on the Kaiser's yacht when the First World War broke out and he never returned to England. During and after the war it became more difficult to run the club, and when Sir Noel Mobbs made an offer for the estate in 1928 it was accepted by 'Pa' Jackson, then 79 years old, and his fellow directors.

Sir Noel Mobbs was one of the founders of Slough Trading Estate. He purchased Stoke Park

57   The winter gardens.

58   The dining room.

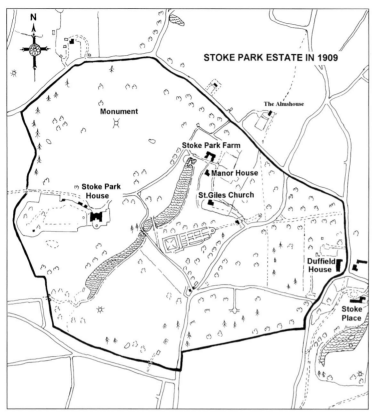

59 Stoke Park Estate in 1909, prior to parts of it being sold for development.

60 The Great Western motor omnibus, 1907.

61 The Mansion and links in the early 20th century.

62 Stoke Poges Golf Club—membership card, 1929.

for £30,000 and lived in part of the Mansion. An enlightened industrialist, Noel Mobbs believed that employers had a responsibility for the social welfare of their employees and a role in the wider community. In 1936 his initiative led to the building of the Slough Community Centre which, with its large hall, social facilities and swimming pool, provided for the leisure interests of some 5,000 members close to where people worked and not far from where many lived. Playing fields were also provided for outdoor games. After the Second World War, his commitment to the provision of health care for employees led to the Slough Industrial Health Service which, in 1948, within a year of being created, was supported by 99 Slough companies employing nearly 11,000 workpeople. Sir Noel also bought the old Manor House near the golf course. He was Lord of the Manor of Stoke Poges and in 1945 became High Sheriff of Buckinghamshire.

In 1958 the Mansion, golf course and other properties were purchased by Eton Rural District Council. It leased the golf course and part of the mansion to Stoke Poges Golf Club 1958 Limited. The remaining floor space was converted for letting as offices. The Manor House with 27½ acres of land, the Gardens of Remembrance, Farnham Park Playing Fields and part of what is now the Farnham Park Golf Course, were gifted to the District Council by the Mobbs Memorial Trust via the Eton Rural District Council Act of 1971.

63 The Club House in 1916.

64 The Manor House as a private residence after it was restored by Dr. William and Mrs. Ellen Morriston-Davies in 1918. In 1921 it was sold to Colonel A.G. Shaw.

Nineteen

Stoke Place and Stoke Green

Stoke Green, now a conservation area with 11 listed buildings, including the long high walls, is one of the older settlements in Stoke Poges. One of the listed buildings probably dates back to the 16th century.

65   The entrance gates off Stoke Road.

The Stoke Place estate with its William and Mary mansion dates back to 1690 when Patrick Lambe bought the land and constructed the three-storey central section of the house sometime before 1698. During this time a feature of the garden was a representation in box of a breakfast given at Stoke to King William and Queen Mary. Later this feature was removed when Capability Brown landscaped the grounds. The east and west wings were added *c.*1755. Further extensions were added during the 19th century, including the two large bow windows.

The long occupation of the Howard–Vyse family began in 1764 when Field Marshal Sir George Howard purchased the house and about thirty acres for £4,300. He also purchased other land at the same time. Sir George was Equerry to Queen

66   Stoke Place, 1999.

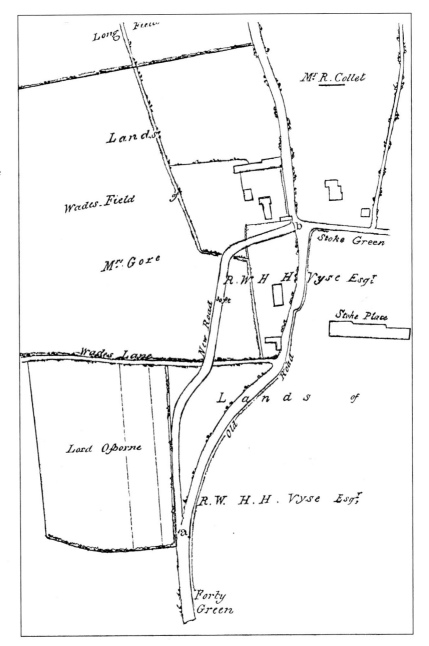

67 Map showing the road diversion *c*.1820.

Charlotte and fought at Fountenoy, Falkirk and Culloden. Sir George's daughter Anne married General Richard Vyse and Stoke Place was inherited by their son Richard William, born in 1784, on the death of his grandfather in 1796. After he married in 1810 Richard William assumed by Royal Licence the additional name of Howard.

Richard William Howard Howard-Vyse was said to have a bad temper and a domineering nature. He was strong minded and conscious of his

68 The Orangery. It is recorded in the Parish Magazine of August 1898 that local children and their teachers were entertained to tea and games at Stoke Place and 'the teachers and visitors were regaled in the Orangery'.

69 Howard Henry Howard-Vyse (1858-1927) as a young officer in the Royal Horse Guards in which he served from 1879-83.

70 Sir Richard Howard-Vyse (1883-1963).

71 Stoke Green.

responsibilities. He played a crucial part in the Stoke Poges enclosure controversy when John Penn sought to enclose Stoke Common. Young Captain Vyse, then in his early 20s, was not afraid of telling Arthur Bold, the vicar, and John Penn, a man twice his age and Lord of the Manor, what their duties were to the poor.

Like John Penn, he extended and improved his estate, and around 1820 he diverted the original Stoke Poges road (now the B416) to the west, further away from his mansion, thus creating the awkward bends in the road (see map). He also built the high brick wall, now an important feature of the conservation area, to keep out 'marauders and vagabonds'. From Stoke House corner the road originally ran through what subsequently became the kitchen gardens of the mansion and then bent round to the

west to rejoin the present road south of the end of the wall.

Howard-Vyse also became an Egyptologist of repute. He wrote a standard work (still consulted) on the Great Pyramids of Gizah. He disinherited his son George because he preferred to marry a lady of his choice rather than his father's. As a consequence the estate passed to his second son Richard. Richard's son Howard Henry (born 1858 died 1927), was very committed to the parish and took an active part in village life. He served as chairman of the Parish Council from 1915 to 1927.

Major General Sir Richard Howard-Vyse, born in 1883, was the last of the family to live at Stoke Place. He had a distinguished military career, serving in Allenby's Palestine campaign in the First World War as Chief of Staff of the Desert Mounted Corps. In 1939, after the outbreak of the Second

72 Stoke Green. The *Red Lion* was built in the 18th century.

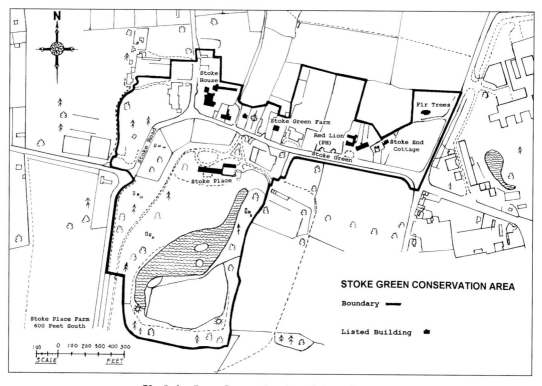

73 Stoke Green Conservation Area, designated in 1986.

World War, Howard-Vyse was sent to France as head of the British Military Mission to General Gamelin. Meanwhile the Duke of Windsor had returned from exile and his future employment presented a problem. He was assigned to Howard-Vyse's Mission and served under him. After the fall of France Howard-Vyse returned to England and became chairman of the Prisoners of War Department of the British Red Cross and St John. This distinguished soldier was High Sheriff of Buckinghamshire in 1938, and he was appointed Deputy Lieutenant in the same year. He was chairman of the Parish Council from 1937 to 1950, and

chairman and then president of the Royal British Legion. Sir Richard died in 1963. In the following year the Stoke Place estate with its 213 acres was purchased by Eton Rural District Council for £93,000. In 1967 a fire seriously damaged the central part of the mansion and despite a temporary roof it was exposed to the elements for 18 months during which time the remaining wings suffered from a severe attack of dry rot and vandalism. It took another 18 months before restoration was completed. It then had various uses and is now a country club.

Twenty
Sefton Park

In the early 18th century Sefton Park was known as Stoke Farm. The 180-acre estate was acquired by the 2nd Earl of Sefton in 1795 as his country seat. A notable Whig who numbered royalty among his closest friends, Sefton, family name Molyneux, was a gigantic 20-stone hunchback with a love of entertaining, hunting and gambling. He is reputed to have lost £200,000 at Crockfords alone during his lifetime. On his death in 1838 the property passed to his eldest son Francis who resided at the family seat at Croxteth Hall in Liverpool, leaving his mother to continue to live at Stoke Farm until her death in 1851.

The 1851 census records that three daughters of the 2nd Earl lived in the house with a household of 31 servants. These included a butler, housekeeper, cook, three ladies' maids, three house maids, two kitchen maids, two laundry maids, a dairy maid, a stillroom maid, a valet, a footman, a coachman, a studgroom, a groom, two stable helpers, a steward's room man, a dressmaker, the head gardener and his servant, four garden labourers and an agricultural labourer. Two of the daughters, Maria and Louisa, never married and a wall plaque in St Giles' Church commemorates them.

Between 1873, when Lady Maria died, and 1905 the house had a succession of tenants and then

74 Sefton Park during the time of the 5th Lord Decies.

75 Vesta Tilley *c.*1906.

76 Eighth Army 'Desert Rat' arm patch.

77 51st Highland Division.

78 Symbol of the Afrika Corps.

owners. The tenants included John George Bulteel, who bought the 10-year-old Grand National winner 'Manifesto' in 1898. The following year, to Bulteel's delight, 'Manifesto' won the Grand National for a second time. The 4th Lord Decies took up residence in 1905. His brother, the 5th baron, completely rebuilt the south wing but this involved him in a long-drawn-out court case because of a dispute with the builder, Holland, Hannen and Cubitt Ltd., over the payment of monies due.

From 1917 until 1922 the house was owned first by Sir Bernard Oppenheimer, the diamond merchant, and then his son. Sir Bernard and his near neighbour, W.A. Judd, were the benefactors responsible for the preservation of Gray's Monument and three acres around it. The next owner was Sir Walter de Frece whose wife Vesta Tilley was the famous music hall star. The book *Recollections of Vesta Tilley*, published in 1934, records how she missed her stage profession. During her resi-

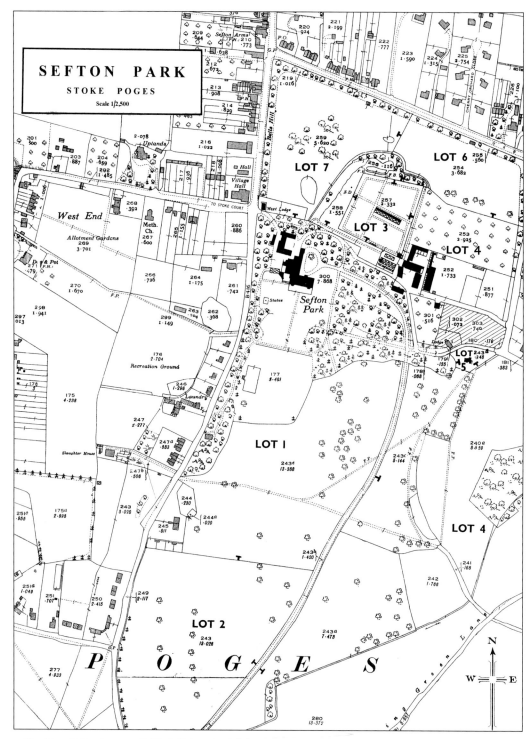

79 The 1948 sale map of the Sefton Park estate showing the land and other properties sold in seven lots. Reproduced from an estate agent's brochure of 1948, Ordnance Survey map by permission of Ordnance Survey on behalf of the Controller of Her Majesty's Stationery Office, © Crown Copyright MC 100031306.

80 The main house, lot one, the entrance hall and the drawing room.

dence from 1922 to 1928 she threw a number of parties in the grounds for local children.

Sir William Duncan and his family owned Sefton Park until 1948 when the house and estate were sold. During the Second World War the house was requisitioned by the War Office and used as a training centre. Its occupants included an American Division, Polish soldiers and, on their return from El Alamein, the 51st Highland Division when they were training for D Day.

The Highland soldiers had brought back a song from Africa, and the story of 'Lilli Marlene' was reported in the *Slough Windsor and Eton Express* on 23 February 1945. Headed 'Dog & Pot Song An Amazing War Story', it read:

The *Dog and Pot* inn at Stoke Poges has become famous overnight in America as the birthplace of a new song. From New York, its licensee, Mr Walter Brigden, has just received a presentation copy of 'Lilli Marlene', the marching song of the Eighth Army, which is

81 South Lodge with entrance gates, lot two.

82 Cottage in kitchen garden, lot three.

sweeping America, together with a copy of *Variety*, the American Magazine, whose front page of 14 October is devoted to the story of how the 51st-Highland Division came home from Africa to its rest quarters near Stoke Poges, and lifted the rafters of the *Dog and Pot* with the German version of the song they had captured on a gramophone record at Tobruk. To the inn came Mr Billy Cotton, the famous dance band leader, and Mr James Phillips, managing director of a music publishing company, who was introduced to a major of the 51st who 'implored him to produce an

English version of the song to stop the boys from singing the German lyric which they had taken over from Rommel's Afrika Corps and made into their theme song'. The song was duly translated into the English version, which is now selling in America at the rate of 600,000 copies in a month.

In 1948, after the death of Lady Duncan, Sefton Park Estate was sold by public auction, being divided into seven different lots. Lot 1 consisted of the main house, with its 22

83 The Home Farm, lot four.

84 Old-world detached cottage known as East Lodge, lot five.

bedrooms, 6 reception rooms and 9 bathrooms, outbuildings and 28½ acres. This was purchased by Glaxo who operated offices and research laboratories until they sold to G.E.C. McMichael in 1982 who, in turn, sold it to the London and Edinburgh Trust in 1989. The house was retained, the Victorian wing demolished and the grounds redeveloped with office blocks creating a business park in a rural setting.

Twenty-One

Stoke Court

During the time of Thomas Gray Stoke Court was known as West End House and was leased to Jonathan Rogers, an uncle of Thomas Gray. His widow Anna became the tenant and she was joined by her two sisters Mary Antrobus and Thomas Gray's mother Dorothy. It was while spending his vacations from Cambridge at West End House that Thomas Gray wrote his 'Ode on a Distant Prospect of Eton College' and his 'Elegy, Written in a Country Churchyard'.

In 1758, after the death of his mother and aunts, Gray gave up the lease and it was occupied by various families, including the Salters, the owners from 1660 to 1828. It was purchased by Granville Penn in 1844. It was Granville Penn's son Granville John who enlarged the house in 1845 and changed its name to Stoke Court. The house was sold in 1851 to Abraham Darby IV, an ironmaster from Coalbrookdale in Shropshire. The Darbys were the famous family who pioneered iron making techniques and had constructed the first iron bridge over the Severn.

The property passed to the Allhusen family in 1872. Christian Allhusen was Danish and of German ancestry. The son of a corn merchant in Kiel, he was only 19 years of age when he emigrated to England in 1825 with just a few shillings in his pocket. He became one of the country's richest industrialists and the chemical works he founded on Tyneside employed 2,500 men. Christian left over £1 million when he died in 1892.

He was succeeded by his grandson Henry. Henry became a member of Stoke Poges Parish

85 Stoke Court when still a private residence in 1921.

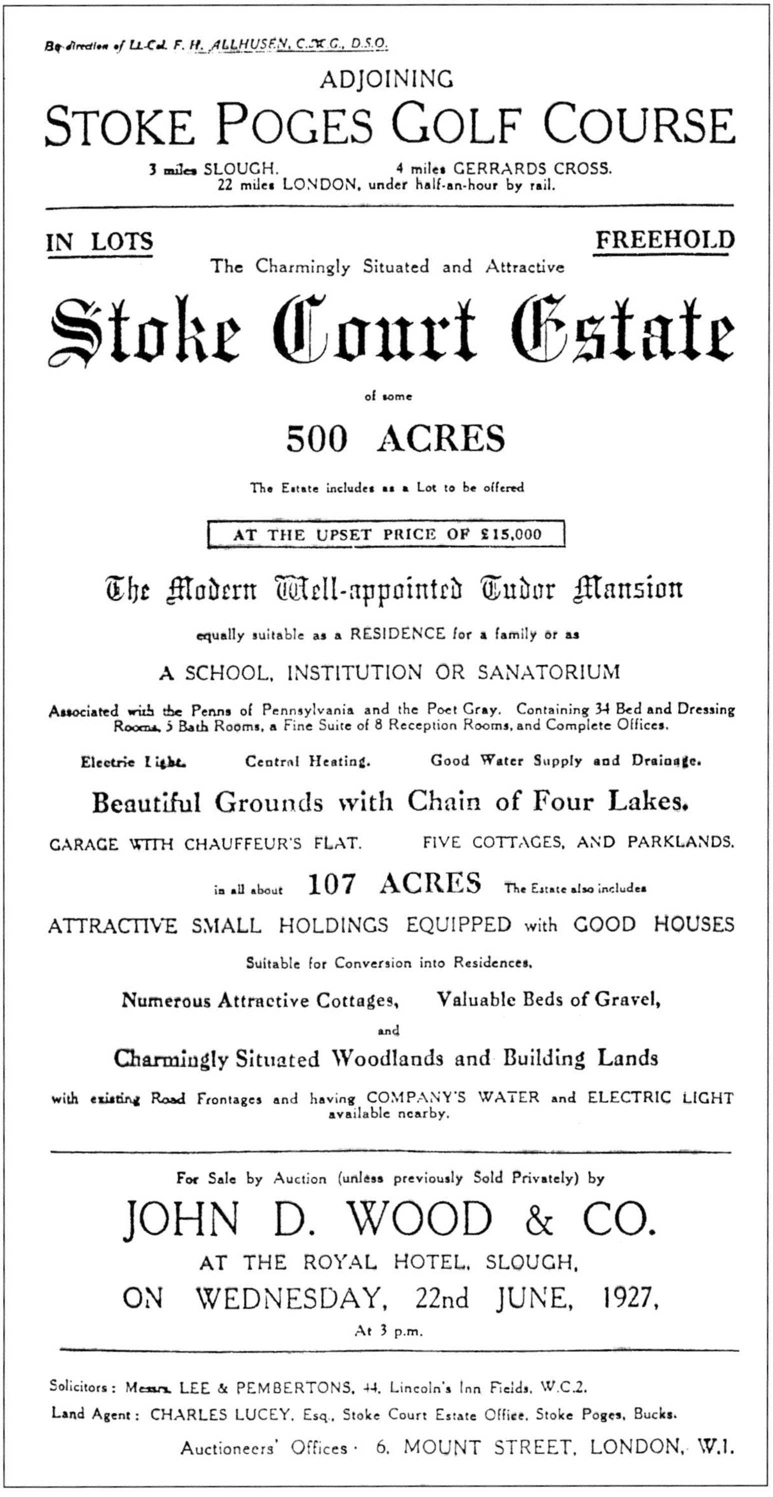

By direction of Lt.-Col. F. H. ALLHUSEN, C.M.G., D.S.O.

ADJOINING

STOKE POGES GOLF COURSE

3 miles SLOUGH. 4 miles GERRARDS CROSS.
22 miles LONDON, under half-an-hour by rail.

IN LOTS **FREEHOLD**

The Charmingly Situated and Attractive

Stoke Court Estate

of some

500 ACRES

The Estate includes as a Lot to be offered

AT THE UPSET PRICE OF £15,000

The Modern Well-appointed Tudor Mansion

equally suitable as a RESIDENCE for a family or as

A SCHOOL, INSTITUTION OR SANATORIUM

Associated with the Penns of Pennsylvania and the Poet Gray. Containing 34 Bed and Dressing
Rooms, 5 Bath Rooms, a Fine Suite of 8 Reception Rooms, and Complete Offices.

Electric Light. Central Heating. Good Water Supply and Drainage.

Beautiful Grounds with Chain of Four Lakes.

GARAGE WITH CHAUFFEUR'S FLAT. FIVE COTTAGES, AND PARKLANDS.

in all about **107 ACRES** The Estate also includes

ATTRACTIVE SMALL HOLDINGS EQUIPPED with GOOD HOUSES

Suitable for Conversion into Residences.

Numerous Attractive Cottages, Valuable Beds of Gravel,

and

Charmingly Situated Woodlands and Building Lands

with existing Road Frontages and having COMPANY'S WATER and ELECTRIC LIGHT
available nearby.

For Sale by Auction (unless previously Sold Privately) by

JOHN D. WOOD & CO.

AT THE ROYAL HOTEL, SLOUGH,

ON WEDNESDAY, 22nd JUNE, 1927,

At 3 p.m.

Solicitors: Messrs. LEE & PEMBERTONS, 44, Lincoln's Inn Fields, W.C.2.
Land Agent: CHARLES LUCEY, Esq., Stoke Court Estate Office, Stoke Poges, Bucks.

Auctioneers' Offices · 6. MOUNT STREET, LONDON, W.1.

86 Auction particulars for the sale on Wednesday, 22 June 1927.

87 The charming residence.

88 The chain of four lakes.

Council along with other members of the gentry when it was first established in 1894. At the time he was only 27 years of age. Two years later he married Mary Stanley at St George's, Hanover Square, receiving a wedding present of a sonnet from the poet laureate Alfred Austin.

Presumably, this was because of Thomas Gray's association with Stoke Court. Henry became a Unionist M.P. but was defeated in the great Liberal landslide of 1906. The visitors' book at Stoke Court contained signatures of the rich and famous of the time including Joseph Chamberlain,

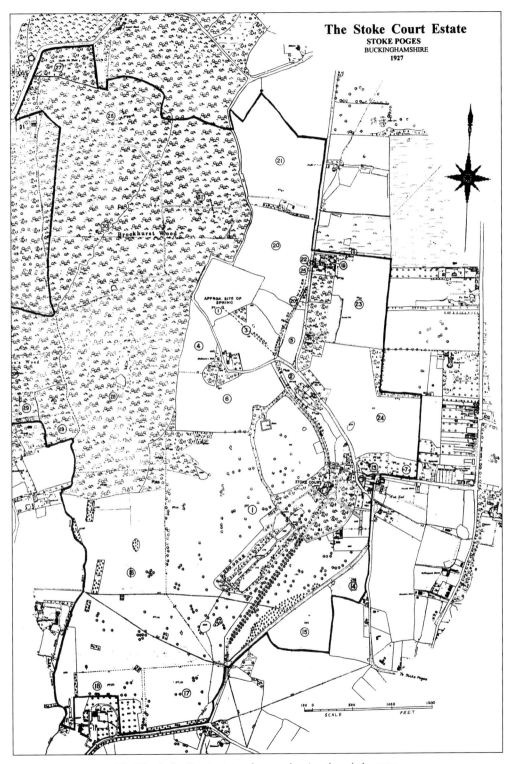

89 The Stoke Court estate sale map showing the whole estate.

90 The main hall.

91 The library.

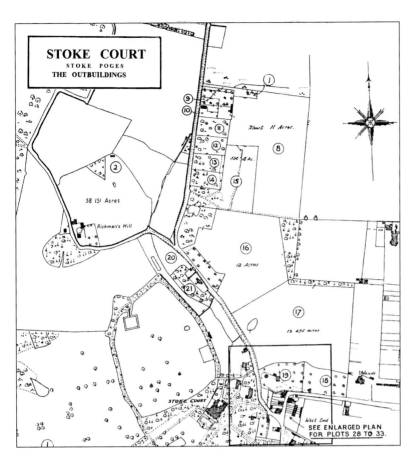

92 Stoke Court estate sale map showing the buildings outside the main residence.

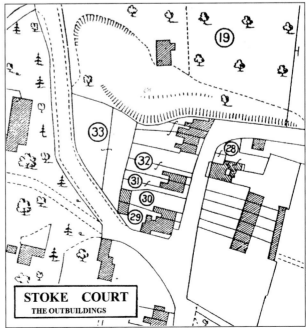

93 Enlarged plan for plots 28 to 33.

94 Stoke Court sale—'Winterclyde', number 28 on the plan. This was described as 'a well built and commodious small double-fronted house, £450'.

95 Stoke Court sale—home number 21 on the plan. 'For easy conversion into a delightful week-end home' with 1½ acres, £650.

The Adjoining Cottage

No. **30** ON PLAN.—The adjoining Cottage which is of similar construction and contains three bedrooms, parlour, kitchen, wash house and outside shed and E.C., together with gardens about 12 poles.   **£225**

————

Note.—The illustration shows adjacent Cottage behind the Car (see former page).

96 Stoke Court sale—an adjoining cottage.

97 Stoke Court sale—two semi-detached houses number 9 on the plan. 'Brick built with slated roof and containing 2 bedrooms, living room, kitchen and wash house. £200. Number 10 on the plan similar to and adjoining same £175'.

98 Stoke Court Country Club.

Winston Churchill, F.E. Smith, Thomas Hardy, John Buchan, Somerset Maugham and John Galsworthy.

Henry died in 1926 but left only £85,487. His younger brother sold Stoke Court the following year, on 22 June 1927, at a public auction at the *Royal Hotel* in Slough, for the 'upset price' of £15,000. All the existing cottages and bungalows, previously occupied by Stoke Court estate servants, were sold. A dairy farm, land suitable for building plots and various parcels of land, including woods, were also sold at the same auction. The house became in turn a private house, a country club and ultimately a warehouse for television sets. In 1958 it had fallen into such disrepair it was to be demolished. Fortunately Miles Laboratories acquired it and restored it. The same company restored it a second time after it was severely damaged by fire in January 1979. It is now the U.K. Conference Centre of the Bayer Group.

99 From inside the building after the fire in January 1979. (Bayer Group photograph.)

Twenty-Two

The Dog and Pot—West End

West End was one of the scattered hamlets and settlements of which Stoke Poges consisted some two hundred years ago. There were twenty or so houses in West End and along what is now the northern bend of Rogers Lane. Just to the west, on the other side of the road from the *Dog and Pot*, was Stoke Court, then known as West End House, one of the four great houses in the parish.

This big house had a marked affect on West End during the 19th century, not only providing employment, but changing its character by a series of road diversions designed to give the house a more spacious setting and greater privacy. By the

100 Richard Holdship's certificate of membership of the Benevolent Brothers Friendly Society in 1879.

time of the first road diversion in 1812 the *Dog and Pot* was a long established alehouse. It served local residents, the brickmakers in the brickfield in Kiln Lane and passing travellers *en route* to Farnham Common and Hedgerley. Called the *Dog's Head and Pottage Pot* in 1758 and the *Dog and Pottage Pot* in 1761, it was first mentioned in the Overseers' accounts in 1787 as the *Dog and Pot*. This was the occasion when it was used as a temporary gaol and 14s. 7d. was paid for a room, bread, cheese and beer for the constable and attendance in taking one William Wilson for whom there was a warrant.

With its six rooms, two downstairs and four bedrooms, with stabling for five horses and a coach house, the *Dog and Pot*, being close to West End House, would have been known to Thomas Gray. It was also one of the centres where payment was made for the destruction of vermin, sparrows and hedgehogs. Between 1792 and 1836 the payment was two shillings a dozen for sparrows. In 1834 some 200 dozen were paid for via Edmund Clarke who was the landlord of the *Dog and Pot* from 1770 to 1810.

There were other serious activities in the tavern for in the previous year, 1833, the Benevolent Brothers Benefit Society was formed. Based in the *Dog and Pot*, by 1875 it had 114 members with an average of £24 14s. 0d. per member. Assets of £2,816 represented a considerable sum for those days. A mutual benefit society providing sickness and other benefits, it operated according to nationally formulated rules. It was no coincidence that it was formed during the incumbency of the Reverend Sidney Godolphin Osborne. He published a number of pamphlets extolling the virtues of thrift by the agricultural labourers through contributions to fuel, clothing and benefit societies and clubs. The Benevolent Brothers were

101   The new *Dog and Pot* in 1900.

supported by their vicar, and the local gentry and farmers were honorary members.

On Whit Mondays the members attended St Giles in procession. In 1838 Godolphin Osborne wrote in one of his pamphlets,

> There are few more delightful sights to those who love the poor than a village club today; – the procession to church, headed by the gentry ... wearing the colours of the club; – the village band, and, O' how they do beat and blow – the flag of which they are proud; – a hundred or two men all in their best, with holiday marked in every face; – the delight of the children, and the pride of the wives and mothers in their Sunday – dressed husbands and sons, makes a picture of happiness and of union for the mutual welfare of many, that does one good to contemplate. I own I am proud of my Club.

By this time, because of a second road diversion in 1832, the *Dog and Pot* was fronting the road to Farnham Common and Hedgerley at the junction of the short road to West End. It was to remain in this location until the end of the century. In

about 1898 Henry Allhusen of Stoke Court, who owned a number of properties on the other side of the road, bought the *Dog and Pot* and pulled it down, diverting the road yet again further to the east and constructing a new drive to Stoke Court. Only the old stables remain today as a charming part of Mulberry Cottage. A new *Dog and Pot* was constructed on its present site on the other side of the road. Allhusen also owned the house in Rogers Lane known today as 'Winterclyde'. Then it was a public house called the *Oddfellows Arms*.

'Winterclyde' has had many uses and has been added to and altered over the years. For a period, around 1846 to 1851, it was the village bakery. It was recorded as such in the parish valuation book of 1846 and described as having '4 rooms, 3 upstairs, a bakehouse, shed, washhouse, stable, loft and cart shed'. The main house, the four rooms and three upstairs, was built around the middle of the 18th century. The single-storey addition at the back was constructed in the 19th century prior to 1846 and

102 The receiving house or sub post office operated from the house opposite 'Winterclyde' from 1847 until 1877. The sub post office, far right, was run by Thomas and Jane Lack and by John Clilverd from 1864 until around 1877 when James Langley was the receiver.

103 James Langley, who from 1861 to 1891 delivered the mail between various South Bucks villages and was the receiver in Stoke Poges in the Parochial Rooms, in Rogers Lane, until the office transferred to Mr. Squibb's store on Bells Hill.

formed the washhouse, stable, loft and cart shed. The existing chimney stack is not original and has been rebuilt above the wider part. Above the porch, which is a very much later addition, is the mark of a chimney, probably the bakehouse chimney, which has been taken down.

In the 1861 census records, the house is described as the police station. After this date it became the *Oddfellows Arms* and in 1876 part of the Stoke Court Estate. A covenant was made as a condition of the sale of the new site for the *Dog and Pot* that the *Oddfellows Arms* should cease to be a public house provided the owner of the new site erected the new public house and finished it within three months of abstracting the deeds.

There were several other shops in this part of Rogers Lane. Opposite 'Winterclyde' there was a receiving house or sub post office. A receiving house had been established at Stoke Green in 1814. In 1830 the inhabitants of West End, led by Lord Doneraile who was renting Stoke Court at the time, asked for a sub post office at West End. The sub

104 West End, now Rogers Lane, *c.*1904. The house with the lady in the doorway was where Mr. Baldwin the postman lived. He was also the cobbler.

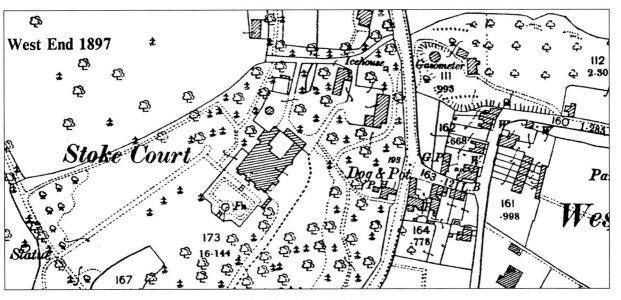

105 Map of West End, 1897.

106 Kiln Cottage was built on part of the old brick kiln and, as a result, was well below the road level. Sited opposite the present school in Rogers Lane, it was demolished in 1973.

107 Two of the four houses built on the site of the old brick kiln during the course of construction in 1973.

108 Poor's Row, six cottages built in 1811, known as Southill Cottages before being demolished in 1972 to make way for Bold's Court, front view.

post office was established shortly afterwards, probably in the old *Dog and Pot*, but by 1847 it had moved into Rogers Lane to the house opposite 'Winterclyde'. It was run by Thomas Lack and later by his wife Jane. From 1864 John Clilverd, a boot and shoe maker in West End, was also sub post master. Whilst there were several other shops nearby, the transfer of the sub post office to James Langley at the Parochial Rooms, formerly the old school house in Rogers Lane, and then to Joseph Squibb's general store on Bells Hill in 1887 started the decline of West End.

109   The rear view of Poor's Row later known as Southill Cottages.

Wilfred Banister recalled his memories of West End just before the First World War—

Further along from 'Uplands' was a pump where the people of West End had to fetch their water. One day a year, I believe on Boxing Day, a rope was hung across the entrance and a man pumped your water. The pump was possibly owned by the Allhusen family. As you carried along Rogers Lane to the corner of West End there was a long shop window house which according to my brother was a general store owned by Mr. Langley although I do not remember it as a shop. Very close to that was where Mr. Baldwin the postman ran his cobbler's business in a shed in his garden. On your left was the police house (Winterclyde). I can remember P.C. Brigginshaw who was highly respected even though he was not above clipping your ear with his gloves or laying his stick where it could be felt. When we came out of Sunday School we used to call at a house in West End occupied by Mr Buckland who sold everlasting sticks and liquorice boot laces, never weighed, so many for a penny.

Twenty-Three

John Thomas Bunby—A West End Character

It was in 1829, when John Thomas Bunby was 14 years old, that the trustees of the Apprenticeship Charity advanced £5 to his father 'to assist him in apprenticing his son John to Bacon, a shoemaker at Slough'. In 1842, then aged 27, John Thomas was listed as a shopkeeper and dealer in groceries and sundries and, in 1847, as a shoemaker and grocer, at West End in Stoke Poges.

his wife Amelia, a son Edward, aged five, and four daughters, the youngest of whom was one year old. A servant lived in with them in the *Dog and Pot*. Although John Thomas Bunby continued as the landlord of the *Dog and Pot* for about twenty years, he had other duties in the village where he was born and where his forebears had lived for generations.

110   West End at the beginning of the 20th century. The house on the corner was Buckland's.

He lived in a house consisting of three rooms, with two upstairs, and he had sheds in which, no doubt, he carried out his craft. This house stood near the old *Dog and Pot* on the south side of Duffield Lane near its junction with Rogers Lane. By 1851 he was the landlord of the *Dog and Pot* and he continued for a time as a shoemaker. He is recorded in the 1851 census with

In 1845, before he took over the *Dog and Pot*, he was first elected assistant overseer for the poor. He held this office, and the offices of assistant surveyor of the highways and surveyor of the highways, for various periods over the next 49 years. He attended the meeting of inhabitants, held in March 1846, to organise a petition to Parliament against the London and Oxford Railway Bill, which proposed the construction of a railway across Stoke Common. However, perhaps his mind was not entirely on this matter because later in the month he resigned his office as assistant surveyor 'in consequence of the smallness of his salary'. This was increased to £16 per annum plus reasonable expenses. He rejected this increase but agreed to continue in office until midsummer. In fact, he continued until 1850, when he was also elected surveyor of the highways at a salary of £25 per annum, on condition he paid £5 of it as a gratuity to the late surveyor, in quarterly payments. Clearly, this was a simple and effective method of superannuation.

For the next few years Bunby held no office, and disputes as to who should fill offices, and whether or not polls should be held, were a regular annual event. This lively form of democracy, and what was called in 1858 'the unpleasantness of constantly agitating the parish by polling it', prompted one person at a meeting to withdraw his proposition for a poll for the office of assistant surveyor of the highways. In the face of Mr. Bunby's threat to propose another candidate, the meeting, with great ingenuity, resolved the problem by abolishing the office for one year. Bunby, however, was elected again as assistant overseer of the poor and held other offices at various times. If out of office he provided critical opposition, as on one occasion when he entered a protest against paying the assistant surveyor of the highways his salary 'on the grounds of his having contracted in the sale of gravel'. He threatened 'to appear before the auditor to oppose the payment'.

In 1871 John Thomas Bunby became a landlord again when he took over the licence of the *Oddfellows Arms* from his son Edward. A few years later he suggested the provision of allotments and he continued to hold parish office until he died in 1894 aged 79 years. In the year of his death parish councils were created. This new form of democracy would have suited John Thomas Bunby, a lively village character.

111 'Winterclyde' was built around the middle of the 18th century or possibly earlier. John Thomas Bunby lived there when it was the *Oddfellows Arms*.

Twenty-Four

The Early Years of the Parish Council

In 1894 Gladstone's last administration changed the vestry system of local government and ended church responsibility for civic functions by creating parish councils and parish meetings in rural areas. The new councils were more democratic and weakened the influence of the squire, gentry and parson. This created new tensions and expectations of improvements as the parish councils used their new powers.

In Stoke Poges the vicar, the Rev. Vernon Blake, had anticipated there would be problems and he had written in the Parish Magazine 'if those who have knowledge in administration will only join hands with those who will bring enthusiasm and self sacrifice to parish work, there is every hope that this last great experiment in the development of better conditions in our villages will be a success'.

The first annual parish meeting to elect a Parish Council of 11 members was held on 4 December 1894 with Vernon Blake in the chair. There were 28 nominations and although the 11 elected by show of hands were representative of the social classes, no one from Stoke in Slough or Ditton, then part of the parish, received enough votes. In accordance with the procedure laid down, the chairman asked if there was anyone who demanded a poll and Arthur Major from Ditton demanded one on behalf of Benjamin Hearn from Stoke Road. It was explained that a poll would cost from £30 to £40 and Mr. Gilliat suggested a committee of five from the north meet a similar number from the other end of the parish with a view to the withdrawal of nominations to avoid the expense of a poll. Mr. Major said the Slough end was not represented and he was not in a position to accept

112 The Reverend Vernon Blake (1828-1901), Vicar of Stoke Poges, 1866-1901.

113 Henry Allhusen.

the suggestion. The chairman said it was his duty to state that a poll must take place.

No poll took place and it was reported in the Parish Magazine that it was subsequently decided to call a private meeting which resulted in 17 candidates agreeing to withdraw, including three of those who had been elected by show of hands. It is not clear why a poll was not held. Once it had been demanded, it was illegal not to have held it. Unfortunately it was to sow the seeds of a bitter row which erupted in early 1896, just before the next parish council election. Then an accusation was made that pressure had been applied to persuade those of lowly status, dependent on the gentry for their livelihoods, to retire.

Yet, following the withdrawals, the resulting membership was a good cross section socially and geographically. There were three gentlemen, Henry Allhusen of Stoke Court, aged 27; Algernon Gilliat, aged 57, a merchant who resided at Duffield House and who later built St Paul's Church and endowed the living; and Edward Parry, aged 38, of Stoke House, where he ran a private school. Parry was elected first chairman from outside the council, a practice permitted at that time. Both Gilliat and Parry were also churchwardens. An indication of the status of these gentlemen was the number of servants each is recorded as having in the 1891 census. Gilliat had six, including a butler, Parry had five and, although the Allhusens were away at the time of the census,

114 Duffield House, the residence of Algernon Gilliat, *c.*1903. Reading from left to right, the first child is probably a Gilliat, the others are Kitty, Una, Margaret and Alastair Easson, whose father, the Reverend Utten Easson, was Vernon Blake's curate and son-in-law.

Local Government Act 1894
P.O. Elec. 33 in List.
HADDEN, BEST & Co.,
West Harding Street, London, E.C.

Members' Declarations on Acceptance of Office.

I, *Henry Eden Allhusen* having been elected PARISH

COUNCILLOR *for the Parish* [or _____ *Ward of the Parish* or *United*

Parishes] *of Stoke Poges* _____

Hereby Declare *that I take the said Office upon myself, and will duly and faithfully fulfil the*

duties thereof to the best of my judgment and ability.

Dated this *31st* day of *December* 189*4*

Henry E. Allhusen

THIS DECLARATION *was made and subscribed before me,*

Algernon Gilliat { *a Member of the*
Parish Council of the
above-named Parish
[or *United Parishes*].

115 The declaration of acceptance of office as parish councillor signed by Henry Allhusen, witnessed by Algernon Gilliat.

presumably with part of their entourage, nevertheless 12 servants remained behind.

The other nine members were Joseph Squibb, aged 55, who was the local postmaster and grocer; Jeremiah Albrow, aged 53, a decorator and plumber who lived in Uxbridge Road; Arthur Ettridge, aged 33 of Hollybush Hill, a gardener and domestic servant who was also a sidesman at St Giles' Church; William Fisk, aged 54, a beer retailer of the *Builders Arms*, Stoke Common; Peter Knight, aged 47, a builder also from Stoke Common and William Stevenson, aged 43, the landlord of the *Sefton Arms*. The remaining three were Arthur Major, a farmer from Ditton and, from the Slough end of the parish, Benjamin Hearn, aged 49, a bricklayer, and Charles Simmons, aged 36, a builder. Both Hearn and Simmons lived in Stoke Road.

116 Charles Simmons, a member of the first Parish Council, was a builder who lived in Stoke Road and, as was the practice at that time, he advertised his business on the front of his house. He built Stoke Road school, the railway bridge and much of Stoke Road north of the railway.

I Admiral Sir John Duckworth (1748–1817), painting by Sir William Beechey, by permission of the Trustees of the National Maritime Museum.

II The Allhusen coat of arms; motto— Foremost if I can.

III Hatchment of Thomas Penn (1701–75), in St Giles' Church.

IV Hatchment of Granville Penn (1761–1844), in St Giles' Church.

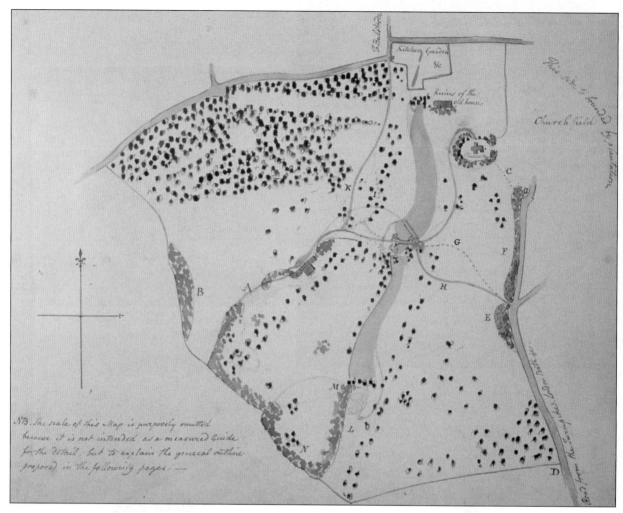

Within the map, the following handwritten labels appear: *To Bulstrode*, *Kitchen Garden &c*, *Ruins of the old house*, *Church Field*, *This side is bound by plantations*, and the letters B, A, K, I, G, F, C, H, E, M, L, N, D.

N.B. The scale of this Map is purposely omitted because it is not intended as a measured Guide for the detail, but to explain the general outline proposed in the following pages.—

V In 1792 John Penn commissioned Humphry Repton to improve Capability Brown's Stoke Park landscape. Repton presented his clients with a book bound in red morocco leather containing water-colour sketches to illustrate his proposals. The Stoke Park 'Red Book' is now in a private collection.

The map above shows how he altered the line of the two approach roads to the Mansion. The road from the Stoke Poges Lane entrance curved to the north but the house was only visible when the bridge was crossed and then only the east end of it. By moving the line of the road to the south before it crossed the bridge, the house and portico appear to the greatest advantage. On the map this change is from dotted line G to line H. The road from the Park Road or Bulstrode entrance was also changed from dotted line I to line K. The effect is also to show the whole of the house, not just the east end. The original road was directed towards the bridge but, Repton writes, 'no road should appear in a park to have any other object than to give easy lines of access to the mansion'. The two sketches opposite show the new views of the house, top using new route H and bottom using new route K.

Repton also sought to improve views from the house including the view to the east and St Giles. Of this view he wrote 'A Church rising out of a plantation is generally a pleasing object, but the same Church surrounded by a brick-wall, looks like the intrusion of alien property'. He therefore sought to create depth and distance across the lake. He used planting 'to give greater prominence' to the spire. This seemingly extended the park to include the church. Repton devised a technique of using a folded flap as an overlay which when lifted shows the changes. In the sketch, overleaf, the top picture shows the flap in place and the bottom one is the same sketch but with the flap lifted.

VI Improved view of Mansion from Stoke Poges Lane approach.

VII Improved view of Mansion from Park Road approach.

VIII View of St Giles before Repton's improvements.

IX View of St Giles after Repton's improvements.

X Stoke Park Mansion, 1890, by B.J.M. Walsh.

XI Ditton Park, the seat of Lord Montague, 1813.

XIII Hatchment of Sir George Howard in the chancel of St Giles' Church.

XII Field Marshal Sir George Howard (1720-96) by Sir Joshua Reynolds. 'A man of stature and proportions largely exceeding the ordinary size … an accomplished courtier and a gallant soldier'.

XIV Stoke Place in the mid-19th century, home of Sir George Howard, and the Howard-Vyse family until 1963.

XV Sefton Park Farm, late 18th century.

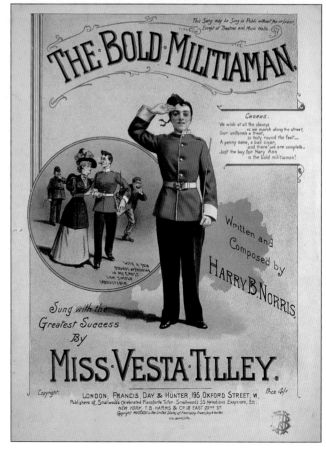

XVI Vesta Tilley—The Bold Militiaman, one of the jingoistic songs prompted by the Boer War.

XVIII Stoke Poges Gardens of Remembrance.

XVII Sir Noel Mobbs, K.C.V.O., O.B.E.

XIX Aerial view of St Giles' Church, 1980, photograph by Chris Stanley.

117 Stoke Road with one of the ten lamps in this part of the parish. In January 1900 Thomas Hatheral, who was paid 18s. 0d. per week for lighting the lamps with oil, was asked to explain his irregularity. He replied that some person or persons nearly every night put out the lamps or broke the glasses. The Parish Council decided 'to have a few bills printed as a caution to persons breaking or injuring lamps' and to ask the clerk 'to call Superintendent Sutton's notice to the matter'. *The Brickmakers Arms* is now called *The Printer*.

The appointment of an assistant overseer (rate collector) and clerk, a joint post at a salary of £50 per annum, was an early and controversial decision. There were two candidates: William Stevenson already acting in an honorary capacity, and Francis Squibb who was the son of Joseph Squibb. Stevenson lost by one vote and, significantly, Joseph voted for his son and Parry voted for Stevenson.

There was already an assistant overseer, Miss Emily Daniels. She had been elected under the old system in May 1894 and had succeeded her grandfather, John Thomas Bunby, who had held the office from 1845 until his death. She was dismissed by the new council because it wished to combine the post with that of parish clerk. Emily did not accept her dismissal without protest and was not going to transfer the books without proper

notice and remuneration for her notice period. She was then given notice and two months salary of £6 13s. 4d.

This presented a problem of where the £6 13s. 4d. was to come from and the gentry had a simple solution which was to deduct it from the new clerk's salary. Francis Squibb objected in what he wrote later were 'words more expressive than polite' but which Parry described as 'gross and literally indecent language to one of the overseers and was such that if there had been ladies on the parish council the matter could not have been discussed in their presence'.

The differences had a political undertone, since the gentry were Conservative and Unionists and some of the parish councillors, including Francis Squibb, were Radicals. This was reflected in the decisions. A request to have a parish nurse was not

118 Stoke House, opposite Duffield House, was a private school where Edward Parry was the headmaster. The school was founded in Clifton in 1867 by the Reverend Edward St John Parry. It moved to Stoke Poges in 1874 and continued as a school until after the First World War when it moved to Seaford in Sussex.

119 The School Room at Stoke House when Edward Parry was headmaster.

followed up, the gentry deciding that it would have to be paid for by public subscription. Henry Allhusen's mother did arrange the funding and organisation. The allotment holders in the Slough end were also concerned about their tenure, fearing they might lose their land, and they asked the parish council to secure it.

Matters came to a head in January 1896 when the Parish Council decided to ask Francis Squibb to resign by 25 March 1896. There was apparent dissent to this decision but when the minutes were presented at the next meeting Parry declined to sign them because they were 'incomplete'. The clerk had not recorded the decision to ask for his resignation. Although four members wanted the minutes signed as recorded, four other members, including Parry, voted to amend the minutes and this was carried on the casting vote of Edward Parry. It was also decided to advertise the post of clerk. At the next meeting, on 18 March 1896, the last before the election, Francis Squibb having failed to post notices of the meeting, particularly the one on the church door, no doubt because the first agenda item was the appointment of a new clerk, Parry asked him to resign. The clerk refused and there was a proposal to dismiss the clerk, with an amendment proposed by Joseph Squibb to postpone the matter until after the election to be held two weeks later. The amendment was defeated by one vote but the voting on the original proposition was equal. Parry declined to give a chairman's casting vote, handed in a letter of resignation and left the meeting.

This dispute was the subject of an acrimonious exchange of correspondence between Squibb and Parry in the two local newspapers in the period up to and after the election. The only member of the gentry to stand for re-election was Henry Allhusen and, of the 16 candidates, 11 issued a joint election address. It read:

'The names of the following candidates are respectfully submitted to you for approval, and if elected, would be suitable representatives of the Parish, being in constant touch with everything pertaining to the "Government of the People - for the People - by the People": Messrs C. Brown, J. Elkins, A.W. Ettridge, W. Fisk, B. Langley, P. Knight, C. Simmons, J. Squibb, T. Templeman, C.T. Wakefield and H.H. Yandell.

Whose utmost endeavour will be to forward the interest of all, and the good and welfare of the parish; they are men who delight in fair play, and will not tolerate party feeling when opposed to the proper administration of Local Government.

Whose interest in the good management of the parish is identical with every rightminded person; they are given to plain speaking, and will aid and assist the working man to obtain all the benefits of the Local Government Act.'

The other candidates were H.E. Allhusen, J.W. Albrow, F.W. Childs, W. Stevenson and J. Hawkins. The result was that eight of the joint signatories of the election address were elected together with Allhusen, Albrow and Stevenson. The balance of power had changed and one of the new members was Thomas Templeman, a plumber, who was the secretary of the Slough and

120 In September 1899 when Jeremiah Albrow was hanging the wallpaper at the newly built *Dog and Pot* he wrote a message on the wall before hanging the paper. This was only revealed when the old paper was stripped off in 1982 prior to redecoration.

121 Advertisements in the Parish Magazine by the tradesmen of 1896.

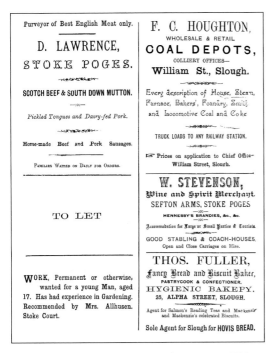

122   Advertisements in the Parish Magazine, 1896.

123   An advertisement for Charles Simmons in the Parish Magazine.

District Radical and Liberal Club in William Street, one side of which was then in the parish.

The new council held its annual meeting on 16 April 1896 and elected Joseph Squibb as its chairman, Henry Allhusen having declined the honour, and Thomas Templeman as vice-chairman. This meeting finally resolved the dispute concerning the clerk. Henry Allhusen outlined the full history and moved the proposal 'That this Parish Council having regard to a resolution by the late Parish Council on January 2nd., and to the fact that the Assistant Overseer and Clerk to the Parish Council did criticise and insult its chairman and members of the Press, does hereby dismiss Mr. Squibb from the posts of Clerk to the Parish Council and Assistant Overseer.' Mr. Templeman urged the council to take a more generous view since Squibb had apologised and he moved an amendment 'That Mr. F. Squibb be retained in the service of the Parish Council and be cautioned to do his duty and that alone under the strict supervision of the chairman and members of the Council.'

Only Allhusen, Albrow and Stevenson voted to dismiss Francis Squibb and after the decision to retain him they handed in their resignations and subsequently Benjamin Langley also resigned. In the following year Henry Allhusen was elected to Parliament and Stevenson and Langley returned to the Parish Council as did Albrow in 1898.

Twenty-Five

Two Stoke Poges Families and the Boer War

Twenty-three men from Stoke Poges fought in the Boer War. From Stoke Court Henry Allhusen's brother Frederick served as a lieutenant. Frederick Ward, who lived in Stoke Court Cottages, then owned by the Allhusens, also served as a sergeant. He took part in the relief of Ladysmith.

In 1900 Mrs. Allhusen entertained to tea the wives and families of Stoke Poges men in the army in South Africa. A photograph was taken of this event. Sergeant Ward's wife Louisa was aged 30 when the photograph was taken and she is the second from the left, in the middle row, holding

her daughter also called Louisa. Next to her is her mother-in-law Mrs. Ball with her other two children Hilda and Wilfred.

Parish records enable us to trace the Ball family back to 1824. In 1824 William Ball, a grocer from Acton, bought a plot of land on Bells Hill two years after it had been divided into a number of plots as a result of the Stoke Poges and Wexham Enclosure Act of 1810. He built a grocer's shop on what is now part of Bells Hill Green. His shop became a branch of the Co-op before the redevelopment of Bells Hill in 1967. It had continued

124 Mrs. Allhusen took this photograph of the wives and families of the men serving in the Boer War when she entertained them to tea in June 1900. The Parish Magazine records 'an elaborate tea was spread for them and a thoroughly enjoyable stroll through the beautiful gardens, visiting the maze and the poet Gray's summer house, was highly appreciated'.

125 Mrs. Henry Allhusen.

126 Wilfred Ward.

127 Certificate presented to Louisa Ward in 1913 by the Royal South Bucks Agricultural Society for keeping her cottage and garden in good order. The Royal South Bucks Agricultural Society still exists. It was founded in 1833 'for the encouragement of industrious labourers and servants and improvements in agriculture generally'.

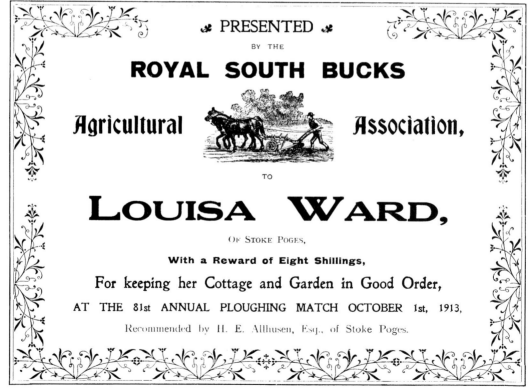

over the intervening years as a grocer, draper and for a period the village post office. William Ball died in 1865 and his son, also William (1823-1898), was the husband of Granny Ball.

The parish records also tell us something about Wilfred Ward, the little boy in the photograph. In March 1915, as senior patrol leader in the scouts, he joined the Local Volunteer Force and proved to be 'a very loyal helper'. In April 1917 the Parish Magazine records 'First Air Mechanic Wilfred Ward has been on leave. Despite the ordinary means of locomotion he seems to have reached our shores on an aeroplane. We wish he had brought it to Stoke and offered the Editor a trip'. Baby Louisa also served in the Women's Royal Flying Corps in the First World War.

At the end of the Boer War the Parish Magazine records the return of Lieutenant Frederick Allhusen to visit his brother at Stoke Court. On 18 July 1900 he was given 'a hearty reception both at Slough Station and in Stoke. A triumphal arch of welcome had been erected at the New Road entrance to the estate, and so enthusiastic were the crowd that they insisted upon taking the horses out of the carriage, and dragging it, with its occupant, up to the house. In the meantime the bellringers, from the old church tower, were ringing a merry peal of bells in honour of his return'. One week later Sergeant Frederick Ward returned and Mrs. Clilverd, of Stoke Park Lodge, received the Queen's Bounty of £4 for having three sons fighting under the flag.

Twenty-Six

The Ancient Parish Changes to the Modern Parish

The ancient parish of Stoke Poges included not only Ditton, but land now part of Slough as far south as the Bath Road including Salt Hill, and land to the west side of William Street and Stoke Road. The area around Stoke Road was known as Stoke in Slough.

Slough was created an Urban District Council in 1894 and boundary adjustments reduced the area and population of Stoke Poges. The first transfer in 1894 was the Bath Road and William Street corner. This was where the *White Hart*, one of the old coaching inns, stood. The site is now occupied by the Slough Central Library and buildings to the west, as well as Thames Valley University. In 1900 an even larger area of land from the Bath Road in the south to a little further north than Baylis House became part of Slough. In 1930 and 1931 Ditton and the area comprising the Baylis Estate and Manor Park also became part of Slough. This completed the expansion of Slough into the parish of Stoke Poges, taking it to the southern boundary of Stoke Park. The area transferred included the route of the Great Western Railway. Slough needed this land to provide housing for its growing population. The development of Slough Trading Estate after the First World War created employment opportunities at a time of economic depression.

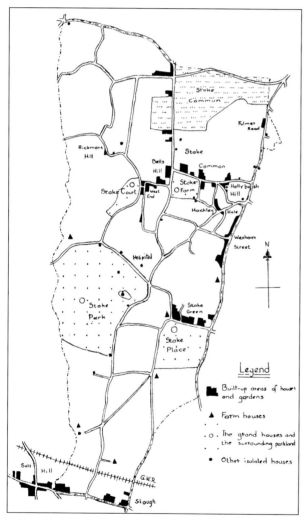

128 The map shows the scattered hamlets of Stoke Poges, the farm houses and the grand houses and surrounding parkland. Ditton, a detached area of 435 acres, was also part of the parish. (Reproduced by permission of Dr. Judith Hunter.)

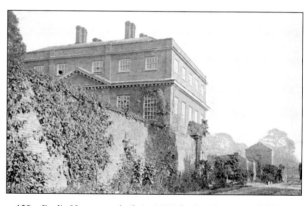

129 Baylis House was built in 1695 for Dr. Henry Godolphin, then Provost of Eton. In 1785 the property passed by marriage to Francis Godolphin Osborne, 5th Duke of Leeds, whose son Sidney became the Vicar of Stoke Poges, 1832-41. It was during the ownership of the last Lord Godolphin that Lord Chesterfield occupied Baylis House for a time. According to tradition he wrote some of his famous 'Letters to his Son' in the library of the house.

130 In 1838 the Great Western Railway from London to Bristol was opened. It crossed the southern part of the parish. In 1846 opposition to the London and Oxford Railway Bill, the route of which was to cross Stoke Common, was successful. Again in 1905, a proposed G.W.R. line from Uxbridge to Burnham Beeches across Stoke Common was also prevented.

131 After the southern part of the parish was transferred to Slough, the agricultural area began to be developed. In 1906 Horlick's factory was built next to the railway line. Within two decades the fields around it were developed with houses.

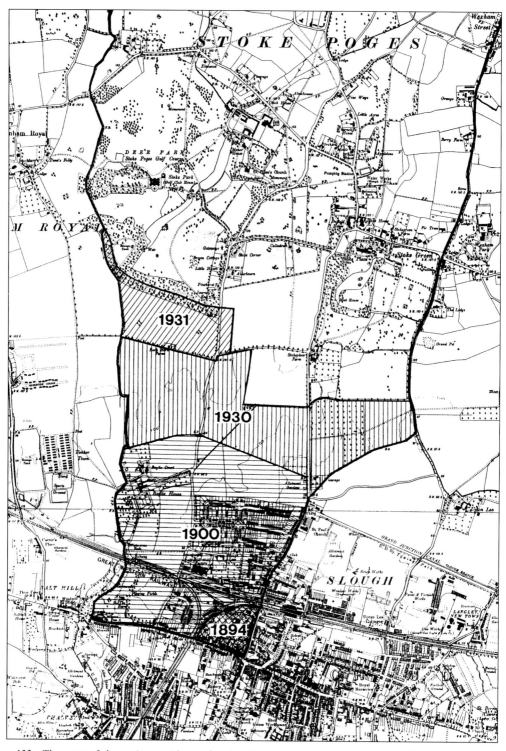

132 The areas of the ancient parish transferred to Slough by boundary changes and then subsequently developed. Ditton was also transferred to Slough in 1929.

133   An agricultural advertisement in 1907 for special corn manure.

The early years of the 20th century were marked by the break-up of the great estates and their redevelopment. The first in 1909 was Stoke Park. The sale of Duffield House in 1926, the residence of Algernon Gilliat and once part of Stoke Park, led to a small avenue now known as Duffield Park. It confirmed a trend and was followed in 1927 by the division of the Stoke Court Estate. As a consequence the commuter population increased although some of the land was not built on until the major population expansion of the 1950s when Stoke Court Drive and Lakeside Drive were built. The last great estate to be sold off was Sefton Park in 1948 and this led to the building of Sefton Paddock and houses on the south side of Hollybush Hill. Substantial housing construction in the 1950s and 1960s completed the post-war expansion of Stoke Poges. Further development is constrained by Green Belt boundaries.

Twenty-Seven

The First World War—Those Who Died

During the First World War the population of Stoke Poges was less than 1,500 people. The Parish Magazine of 1919 records that 302 villagers answered the call and joined the services. Of this number 48 were killed or died of their wounds and, like countless other villages and towns throughout the country, their names were set on a memorial as a public and continuing witness to ensure that succeeding generations are mindful of what has gone before.

Stoke Poges War Memorial takes the form of a tablet of Hoptonwood Stone and is positioned on the north chancel wall of St Giles' Church. It was installed at a cost of £360 18s. 0d., raised by donations from the village, and dedicated by the Dean of Windsor on Sunday, 4 January 1920. The Memorial encompasses the tragedy of the Great War and the demands made upon the folk of a small village. Although members of infantry regiments predominate, those included were members of the Royal Navy, Royal Marines and the Royal Air Force as well as Army. Their ages ranged from 18 to 42. They lie buried or commemorated in France and Flanders, Gallipoli, Egypt, Palestine and Salonika as well as the U.K.

Of the 48 men listed, 14 have no known grave. Throughout each of the years of the Great War there was at least one family connected with Stoke Poges which received news of the death of a husband, son, father or brother.

The worst year of the war was 1917, the year of the struggle to take Passchendaele, when 18 men from Stoke Poges died. The roll includes one man killed on the first day of the Battle of the Somme, the worst day in the history of the British Army when 57,470 British soldiers became casualties, a number that exceeded the

134 The First World War Memorial.

totals of British battle casualties of the Crimean, Boer and Korean Wars put together. Five families from Stoke Poges suffered the loss of two members including three pairs of brothers. One of these pairs, William and Reginald Clifton, forms the basis of an unusual link between St Giles' and St Andrew's Churches. In the entrance to St Andrew's is mounted a stained glass window commemorated to the brothers. This originally formed part of a window in St Wilfred's Chapel, which stood until 1973 in Chapel Lane.

The younger brother, Reginald, joined the Royal Army Medical Corps in February 1915 and subsequently transferred in March 1917 to the 1st/6th Battalion of the Manchester Regiment. This Battalion was involved in an advance on the Somme on 21 August 1918 which proved to be only partially successful. On that day the Battalion lost one officer wounded, 15 other ranks killed and 24 other ranks wounded. That was the price for the limited amount of ground gained, some fifty prisoners captured and six light machine guns taken. Private Clifton, aged 20, was one of those killed and lies in Queens Cemetery, Bucquoy.

Private Clifton's elder brother William volunteered as a trooper in the City of London Rough Riders at the outbreak of the war and was subsequently wounded at Gallipoli in August 1915. It was in that month that he was commissioned into the 3rd Battalion, Oxford and Bucks Light Infantry. On 30 December 1916 Lieut. Clifton joined 11 Squadron RFC in France as an Observer. Records have not survived to show how many times Lieut. Clifton flew but it is possible to piece together the details of his last flight.

No.11 Squadron was a reconnaisance unit flying the FE2b, a two-seater biplane with its engine mounted to face the rear in order that the observer in the front cockpit had the widest possible vision and to provide the maximum field of fire for the two Lewis guns he manned. At 6.20 a.m. on 31 March 1917, 6 FE2bs took off

135 Stained glass in the entrance hall of St Andrew's Parish Centre, Rogers Lane, Stoke Poges, commemorating the Clifton brothers.

to rendezvous with 4 Nieuport fighters of 60 Squadron which were to act as escorts. During the patrol over enemy territory the formation was attacked.

In a letter to *Popular Flying* published in April 1934, the pilot of FE2b No.7691 Lieut. L.A. Strange explained, 'I was shot down by Lieut. Wolff of the Richtofen Circus on the morning of 31 March 1917 at Gayrelle. I regret to say that the first burst from Wolff's guns mortally wounded my observer, Lieut. Clifton, and almost immediately afterwards

136 An armed two-seater FE 2b reconnaissance biplane. (Reproduced by permission of the Imperial War Museum.)

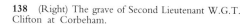

137 (Above) Royal Flying Corps shoulder patch and cap and lapel badge.

138 (Right) The grave of Second Lieutenant W.G.T. Clifton at Corbeham.

my engine cut out owing to the tank being riddled with bullets. It was necessary to tip the machine up on her nose in order to lift Lieut. Clifton out'.

Lieut. Strange, himself wounded, was taken prisoner. A letter he wrote whilst a prisoner to his father was the evidence accepted of Lieut. Clifton's death. William Clifton lies in a small plot containing just eight graves maintained by the Commonwealth War Graves Commission within a communal cemetery at Corbeham, a village to the south west of Douai. Kurt Wolff went on to amass 33 air combat victories before he, almost inevitably, met his own death in action on 15 September 1917.

These are but two instances of the tragedies borne by folk of Stoke Poges during the Great War. Behind each name on the Memorial lies a story to be told of those prepared to lay down their lives and were called upon to pay the price.

Twenty-Eight
Fred Spring of Stoke Green

Fred Spring lived in a cottage next to the *Red Lion* in Stoke Green. He was a gardener on the Howard-Vyse estate and he died in 1970. In the First World War he served in France in the Oxford & Bucks Light Infantry and survived 16 days lying in No Man's Land. Here is what he wrote to Canon Barnett who was vicar of Stoke Poges at the time:

> You said you would like to have an account of my experience of 16 days lying out in No Man's Land, which I can assure you was a most weird and unpleasant one.
>
> Our Company went up to the trenches on the 2nd May, 1917, and about 12 of us went on patrol all night, and came back at 3 a.m. to report, and then we made an attack on Fritz.

I was wounded just after half-past 3, while running across to get at Fritz, and was shot twice through the leg, one bullet passing through and one staying in, causing a compound fracture. I crawled in a shell-hole close by, and there I lay, with several more, until night fell, when they all crawled away except three of us, one with his foot nearly off, one wounded in the leg and back, and myself.

We waited and prayed that stretcher-bearers might find us and pick us up, but nobody came until three days afterwards, when a Sergeant found us. He told us he would send us help and that the R.A.M.C. was coming to search for us. But as he was speaking to us the shelling was fast and furious, and there did not seem much chance of anyone reaching us, as both sides were

139 The St Giles' Church ringing team of 1913: from left to right—J.J. Parker (of composition fame), A. Bateman, Fred Spring, Canon A.T. Barnett (vicar), W.T. Bateman, W. Henley, J.L. Bateman and F. Tarrant (verger). Not in photograph E. Garbett.

sweeping the ground with shells, so we kept each other as cheerful as we could. What little food we had we were obliged to be very careful with, but water seemed to be the worst trouble. We had none for days; in fact I never tasted water for eight days.

After eight days of weary waiting in the first shell-hole, two of us said we would try and crawl to our lines. So while I was getting out of the shell-hole the other one crawled a little way and found half-a-bottle of water and a 'Machonocie',[1] which we gave to the one with his foot nearly off. We then started off and got about 50 yards when my mate said he could go no further, and we had found nothing to eat and drink. Soon I saw a poor fellow about 20 yards away, and decided to see what he had on him, but when I got to him I found nothing, so crawled a little further to another, and found three parts of a bottle of water and a little food. I had some difficulty to find my mate in the shell-hole again, and just as I got back and safely in, machine gun bullets came whistling right over the shell-hole, so Fritz must have seen me and

140 The peal board in the bell tower recording the farewell peal to Edward Parry.

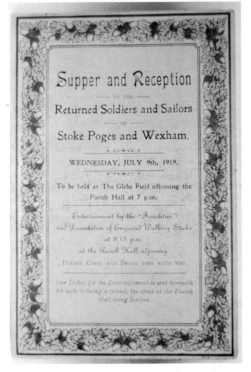

141 Supper and reception to the returned servicemen and list of hosts and hostesses.

142   The returned servicemen photographed in front of Gray's monument in 1919.

143   The row of seven terraced cottages in Stoke Green where Fred Spring lived. Built in the 19th century, they were part of the Howard-Vyse estate.

it made me feel jolly queer I can tell you.

We decided to stay where we were for one more night and try our luck the next night, but we felt too weak and ill, so we had to stop four days with only the three parts of a bottle of water. My mate then said he felt better and would try to get in, but I am sorry to say that half-an-hour later the poor fellow died. So I stayed there until 10 o'clock at night and then tried to crawl in, but what with the shelling and the shell-holes I made no headway, but only kept knocking my leg against great clots of clay, which caused me intense pain and made me feel ill.

I stopped for a rest in another shell-hole, in which were two more chums, and I found a bottle of water and a little food on one of them. It seemed little enough, and I had to look at it to see whether I dare eat any. I managed to make it last by allowing myself about three dessert spoonfuls a day and eating grass and dandelions in between whiles. Thank God it rained one day, and I was able to catch one bottle of water, which lasted me until the night I got picked up.

Fritz was on the look-out all the while for moving objects, and he spotted a patrol of ours, and there was a tidy old dust-up for a while. At 10 o'clock that night I felt as if I ought to make a last attempt to find our trenches, which I thought lay about 300 to 400 yards away, so I started to crawl along as best I could. It was slow progress, and my leg pained cruelly, but I stuck it, and reached our lines at 2 a.m.

They gave me something warm to eat and drink and made me as comfortable as they could for the time being, and by stages I got to hospital and from there to Blighty. It seemed good to see the trees and flowers once more instead of ruin and havoc everywhere. I could write a lot more, but I am afraid I have made it too long as it is, so will dry up. F. Spring.

Fred Spring was a bellringer and illustration number 139 shows him third from the left in the St Giles' Church ringing team of 1913. The occasion was a peal of 720 of Oxford Bob Minor rung on the new bells as a farewell to Edward Parry who had been a churchwarden for 30 years.

Twenty-Nine

Gray's Meadow is Saved

Until after the Second World War there was no planning legislation to protect the countryside from builders. Only the initiative of public spirited citizens could preserve the best from undesirable development. Gray's Meadow, the 'lea' of the Elegy, was saved by such action when on 5 May 1925 the field was handed over to the National Trust. The deeds were received by Lord Grey of Falloden on behalf of the Trust at a ceremony on the meadow itself. The story of this achievement was recorded in the *Slough Observer*'s report at the time:

> This ceremony marks the completion of, perhaps the most important stage in an effort which has been prolonged over a period of nearly ten years. In 1912 Canon A.T. Barnett was appointed vicar. He soon perceived that there would roll upon Stoke Poges, in common with all other pleasant districts near to London, the tide of building which nothing seems to stop. That this, should it reach the edge of Gray's churchyard, would be intolerable was apparent. Modern houses and bungalows, inoffensive or even beautiful as they might be, directly overlooking the 'ivy mantled tower', 'the rugged elms', the 'yew trees' shade', the turf that heaves 'in many a mould'ring heap', would be so utterly out of harmony with the spirit of the place that it was not to be thought of.
>
> Accordingly Canon Barnett made foresighted plans to prevent the threatened evil. His first chance came when, some years ago, access was restricted by a gate across a right-of-way. He fought that cause, and won it, and out of the victory came the great idea. Stoke Poges Churchyard lies remote from the road. It is approached by a short lane, and, stretching away from the lane to the corner of a road that almost encircles Stoke Park, is the pleasant bit of meadow land, checkered with elms and a few firs, and ringed by a beautiful coppice-hedgerow of characteristic English timber and undergrowth, in which stands Wyatt's huge cenotaph, commissioned by John Penn in memory of the poet. That meadow secured from building meant continued seclusion. Delivered over to building, all that made Stoke Poges reminiscent of the Elegy was sacrificed for ever. It is in itself delightfully rural.
>
> It is this beautiful meadow that has been secured. First, the nearest three acres of it, with the Penn memorial, were bought and presented by the late Sir Bernard Oppenheimer and Mr. W.A. Judd. That, temporarily, held the breach. On the death of Sir Bernard Oppenheimer, the remaining ten acres came into the market. Canon Barnett and Mr. Judd bought this portion for £2,000. They might have sold it since for £4,000 or £5,000. Instead, they have held it - without charge for interest - until the money could be raised. To the new Parochial Church Council was given the opportunity of carrying through the appeal, always with the devoted help and initiative of the vicar, and it is on behalf of that council that the deeds are to be handed over.

There were two appeals for a total of £6,000 to purchase the land and repair the tower of St Giles. The appeal committee sought the support of many eminent men and asked them to write letters to the *Daily Telegraph*. The correspondents included G.K. Chesterton, John Buchan, Anthony Hope-Hawkins, A.E.W. Mason and Edmund Gosse, Gray's biographer. Of those who subscribed it was said, in its roster of noble names, the subscription list was like a court calendar, with a

144 The 'lea' of the Elegy.

duke, three marquises, four earls, two viscounts, two lords, ten ladies and four baronets. Mrs. Winston Churchill, Leslie Henson and Walter de la Mare were also subscribers in a list which ranged from Master Sharp's one shilling to a Mrs. Fortune of the U.S.A. who sent 2,000 dollars, or £400 at the then exchange rate of five dollars to the pound, a quite substantial gift.

Of the ceremony on 5 May 1925, the *Slough Observer* wrote that it was 'a red letter day in Stoke history' and 'the consummation of a noteworthy achievement, upon which Canon Barnett and his hard working committee are to be sincerely congratulated'. Today, we have every reason to remember with gratitude the foresight, energy and generosity that saved the lea of the Elegy from development and preserved an important part of our heritage.

145 Gray's monument was designed by James Wyatt and erected by John Penn in 1799. The large stone pedestal has four panels inscribed with verses from the 'Elegy'.

146 A large gathering, including many local people, at the ceremony on 5 May 1925 when the deeds were handed over to the National Trust.

Thirty
Stoke Poges Gardens of Remembrance

147 The stone recording that Sir Noel Mobbs founded the Gardens.

Stoke Poges Gardens were the inspiration of Sir Noel Mobbs. He had the foresight to see that this land near the church of Gray's Elegy, and formerly part of Stoke Park, could be acquired for housing development. He therefore purchased the land to preserve the setting of St Giles' Church and to create the Gardens as an oasis of peace and tranquillity, a quiet place for contemplation. They were constructed under the direction of Mr. Edward White, the noted landscape architect, who designed the area so that individual gardens were created within the overall concept which preserved all the natural features. The individual gardens and

148 The Bishop of Buckingham dedicated the Gardens of Remembrance on 25 May 1935.

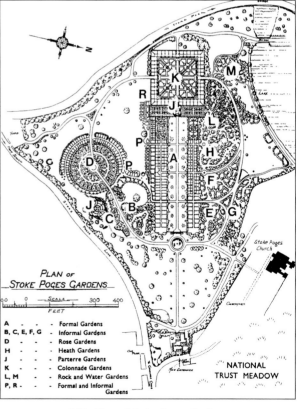

149 Plan of Stoke Poges Gardens.

150 Leading to the Colonnade.

151 The old bell, said to be the 'curfew' bell of the Elegy, when it was displayed near Church Cottage.

152 Church Cottage, where the sexton lived, from the east, front entrance, late 1920s. A 16th-century building, it was extended in the 20th century with a two-storey addition on the east side.

153 Church Cottage in 1930, also from the east.

154 The Gurkha Memorial.

plots were provided for the private interment of cremated remains. The Gardens were dedicated on 25 May 1935 by the Bishop of Buckingham. In 1971 ownership of the Gardens was transferred by a Private Act of Parliament to the District Council who are required by the Act to continue to maintain the Gardens to the same high standards as applied from their creation in 1934 to the time of the transfer.

There are about 2,000 individual gardens in about 20 acres in this serene setting. It contains all types of traditional gardens, including rose, heath, parterre, colonnade, rock and water, formal and informal. The main avenue leads down to the colonnade which is a splendid feature with its columns, water channels, magnolia trees and colourful flower beds. The plots where ashes are interred are marked only by small plaques. There are also many fine trees, some of great age, with one in particular in the Dell reputed to be 600

155 Church Cottage *c.*1930, the Penn-Gray Museum, south view from the Gardens.

years old. One of the individual gardens, consecrated in 1949, is a memorial to all ranks of the Gurkha Regiment who gave their lives in service between 1857 and 1947. An annual Remembrance ceremony is held each year in June by the Gurkhas to honour their past members.

Church Cottage near the entrance to the Gardens used to be the headquarters of the Penn-Gray Society and is now the administrative centre for the Gardens. An old bell inscribed 'Robert Gayer Esquire 1660', formerly in the gardens of the cottage, is now exhibited in the Penn Gray Museum in the South Bucks District Council Offices. This bell is reputed to be the curfew bell that 'tolls the knell of parting day', in Gray's Elegy. Robert Gayer was

the Lord of the Manor who refused to admit William of Orange to the Manor House. The urn to the memory of Lady Juliana Penn, mother of John Penn, which also used to be in the cottage gardens, has been moved to the lawn near the lake. Here it commands a splendid view of Stoke Park Mansion.

In 1996 these unique Gardens were placed on the English Heritage Register of Parks and Gardens of Special Historic Interest in England and are Grade II listed. There are fine views from the Gardens to the Repton Bridge, Stoke Park Mansion, the lake, the Manor House and the restored landscape of Stoke Park.

Thirty-One
Stoke Park Conservation Area

In 1986 the landscape embracing Stoke Park golf course with its mansion, the playing fields to the south, the Manor House and grounds, the Gardens of Remembrance, Gray's Meadow, together with St Giles and the churchyard, was designated as a conservation area.

The District Council acquired Stoke Park in 1958 but was unable to find enough money for maintenance or upkeep and, initially, had little interest in conservation. Repton's bridge, owing to lack of timely repair and vandalism, was one example of a general decline. Interest in the need for conservation began to develop from 1982 when the Council leased the old Manor House to the Dana Corporation of Toledo, Ohio. Dana paid £455,000 for a 99-year lease and spent a consid-

erable sum on overdue maintenance. The London Landscape Consortium prepared landscaping proposals, and plans were approved for a linked extension to the old house.[1]

Stoke Poges Parish Council pressed the District Council to designate Stoke Park as a conservation area in order to halt further decline and raise standards. Although the area designated in 1986 includes ten listed buildings, it is the landscape design that holds all these elements together. Architecturally the buildings are important but it is their historic and literary associations within the landscape that are so unique.

In the same year, realising that the golf club lease had only seven years to run, the District Council made the future preservation of Stoke Park

156 The Manor House.

mansion a priority. The success with the Manor House led to the conclusion that conversion to total office use, and a long lease to a commercial user with the resources to preserve the fabric, was the way forward. Two years before this decision I.H.G., the International Hospitals Group, had taken over the tenancy of the offices in the mansion. In 1988 their offer of £2 million for a 250-year lease was accepted. I.H.G. undertook to spend what was required to repair the fabric and restore the grounds.

The District Council had commissioned Land Use Consultants, advisers to the Royal Parks, to recommend what was required to restore the east vista. I.H.G. asked the same consultants to do more detailed work on Stoke Park which included restoration of vistas, views and the historic gardens. The resultant research and further work in 1991 radically changed I.H.G.'s view of what was required to return the estate to its former glory. It was decided not to implement the office conversion planning consent but to return to the 1908 country club use. This could generate the revenue needed for viability but would require an investment of up to £30 million.

The golf club lease expired in 1993 and a new proprietary club was formed with an amicable handover. Most of the members and all the staff joined the new organisation. The future plans were given further impetus in 1996 when Stoke Park as a whole was listed Grade 1 on the English Heritage Register of Parks and Gardens of Special Historic Interest. Since then the top two floors of the mansion have been reinstated to the 1790 Wyatt bedroom layout and there are now 21 bedrooms, four conference rooms and a shop and restaurant. Considerable work has been completed on landscape restoration including the 14 acres of historic gardens. With the purchase of a further 100 acres, the 9-hole golf course ploughed up during the Second World War has been recreated. The additional 9 holes, opened in March 1999, give a

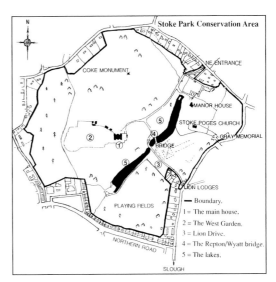

157   The Conservation Area.

27-hole facility based on the original Colt design of 1908.

A new Health and Racquets building, incorporating indoor tennis courts, a swimming pool and a gym, will be opened in June 2001. This will follow the restoration of Repton's Bridge. As a result of the cooperation of all the parties with an interest in the conservation area, the District Council, St Giles' Church, the National Trust, Crane Davies of the Manor House, I.H.G. and the Parish Council, a new Heritage Walk has been opened and vantage points provided to give public views of historic buildings and restored vistas.

158   Restoring the views of the past where practical.

Thirty-Two

Schools in Stoke Poges

The first reference to education in Stoke Poges is in 1716 when Mary Salter of West End House left £100 in her will 'for teaching poor children of the parish to read, write and cast accounts'. Her sister Margaret Todd also bequeathed £100 in 1717. There were other smaller gifts making a total of £235, and in 1731 a Trust was formed by the vicar and six parishioners. The Trust bought cottages and eight acres of land at Morralls End, roughly the site of Bells Hill Recreation Ground. In 1751 the first village school was built on the lower part of Sefton Park.

There were three further bequests; in 1791 Mrs. Mary Church left £130 0s. 4d. worth of 3 per cent Consols, in 1812 Mrs. Parker Sedding in her lifetime gave £336 6s. 8d. in Old Southsea Annuities and in 1831 the Reverend Arthur Bold left £50 in 3 per cent Stock. In 1800 a new school was built in Rogers Lane at a cost of £101 and it was extended in 1842. It still stands today, was used as the Parish Rooms in the 1920s and now it is divided into three cottages.

By 1817 the schoolmaster, G. Armstrong, who was paid £20 per annum with a house and garden

159   The old school house built in 1800.

160   The school built in School Lane in 1876.

161　One of the classes of 1908.

162　Maypole dancing, May Day 1912.

provided, had 70 pupils: 30 'foundation' children (presumably educated under the Trust), 10 paid for by a contribution of £6 10s. 0d. from the parish rates, and 30 paying pupils. Those taught free nevertheless had to make a small contribution: some one penny and others a halfpenny per week.

The school was conducted on the national system which meant it belonged to the 'National Society for Promoting the Education of the Poor in the principles of the Established Church'. It abided by the standards set by the Society. By 1839 the school is recorded as having room for only 30 boys and 30 girls. There were two other infant schools, one maintained at the private cost of the Ladies Molyneux (daughters of the Earl of Sefton) and the other for 16 children provided by Miss

Vyse. Two or three Dame schools were run in private homes by women, usually widows, to secure a livelihood.

Government grants were available to National schools and from 1862 grants were dependent on satisfactory reports on examination of performance, attendance and accommodation. One requirement was that log books should be kept. These still exist, dating from 1862, and are kept at the County Record Office in Aylesbury. An early entry recorded the granting of a half-day holiday on the occasion of the marriage of the Prince of Wales (later Edward VII) in 1863. The log books also recorded many a sally by the teachers after truants. Boys are recorded as being absent for various reasons including acorn

163　Stoke Poges girls, group 3, teacher Miss Sergeant, 1919.

164　Class of 1928, teacher C.D. Webb.

165 & **166** Stoke Poges First School playtime, 1976.

gathering, stone picking, hay making and beating for shooting parties. In one case the school terminated at 11 a.m. because of a stag hunt. The Education Act of 1870 established a countrywide system of elementary education supported by local rates with school boards. By this time the Stoke Poges school had become overcrowded and a

meeting of ratepayers was called in 1871 to consider enlarging the school. Instead it was decided to build a new school. Plans were approved to build a new school at a cost of £2,527 to accommodate 310 children. The local Trust felt unable to meet the requirements for a new school and in 1874, two years before the new

167 The First School Centenary, 1976—the staff in Victorian costume. Left to right—Jill Holmes, Gillian Sibbling, Joyce Clark, Margery Tate, Joyce Boxall, Glenys Thomas, Eve O'Sullivan (head teacher), Adele McNally, Brenda Royal and Margaret Tregurtha.

168   Centenary celebrations presentation of painting to the school.

169   Children playing Victorian games, Centenary 1976.

school was built, a School Board was instituted for the United Parishes of Stoke Poges and Wexham.

The trustees of the Charity School had received two allotments of land under the Enclosure Award of 1822. These two parcels were in different parts of the parish but were exchanged for two adjacent plots with a total area of 1 acre 2 roods and 27 perches. This was described in the Award as 'part of an old inclosure called Lashes Field'. The west and south boundaries were 'the lane leading from Stoke Common to Hockley Hole'. Then called Hazel Lane, after the new school was built in 1876 it became School Lane.

The 1870 Act gave school boards the power to enforce attendance between the ages of 5 and 13 years or such ages as they might decide. Stoke Poges decided on an upper age of 12. Although from 1876 the age limit could be raised to 14, the Board stuck to 12, raised it to 13 in 1894 and 14 in 1901. Fees had been fixed in 1863 at 2d per week for parishioners and 4d. for others. In 1891 education became free. Mr. and Mrs. Fellows had been appointed headmaster and headmistress in

1874 and they moved to the new school when it opened in 1876. In 1883 they left to be replaced by Mr and Mrs Batten who were to stay until 1916, the school having become the responsibility of Bucks County Council in 1902. In 1918 the age limit was fixed at 14.

The next milestone was the Education Act of 1944 which reclassified schools as primary and secondary. In 1961 Stoke Poges School became a primary school with pupils up to the age of 11. This upper age was raised to 12 subsequently and is now 11 again. In 1968 a new middle school was built in Rogers Lane adjacent to the old 1800 building. Thereafter the two schools operated separately from two sites—the First School with the 5 to 8 year olds and the Middle School with the 8 to 12 year olds.[1] In 1976 the First School celebrated its centenary with an exhibition, first-day postal cover and other events. The staff and pupils dressed in Victorian clothes and recreated the early years of the school. In 1996 the two schools were combined under one headteacher though still operating from two sites.

Thirty-Three
The Development of Bells Hill

Until 1822 the land north of Rogers Lane and Bells Hill was part of Stoke Common. The Enclosure Award redistributed some three-fifths of the common to landowners in lieu of their common rights. These allotments of land were in proportion to the area of existing land ownership.

Eleven very small landowners received their allotments on Bells Hill. These were ideal plots for development in what became the centre of the village on the main road from Slough in the south, at its junction with the Bath Road, across Stoke Common to Gerrards Cross and the Oxford Road in the north. The church was also allotted a large corner plot fronting Bells Hill and Rogers Lane. Within two decades cottages, two public houses and shops had been built.

The old *Five Bells* had been located at the bottom of the hill in what is now Sefton Park opposite the village pond, now part of the Bells Hill Recreation Ground. It was moved to the top of the hill after 1822, when Thomas Brent was the landlord. However, Sarah Mason also built a public house halfway up the hill sometime after 1824, when the sixth bell was added to the church peal,[1] and called it the *Six Bells*. As a consequence the *Five Bells* was renamed the *Sefton Arms*. Both

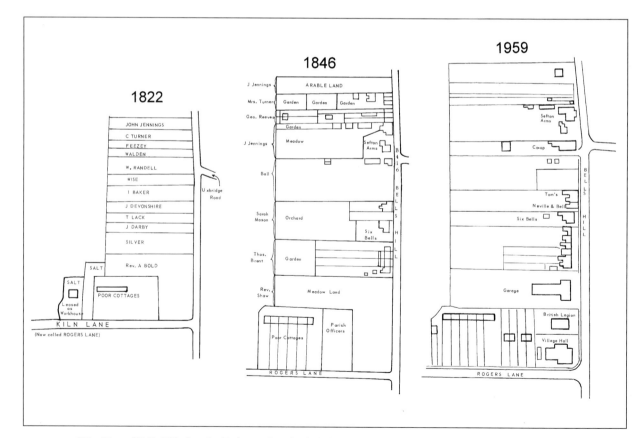

170 Map of Bells Hill after the Enclosure Award of 1822, as recorded in a valuation map of 1846 and in 1959.

171 The village hall soon after it was built in 1912.

172 Looking north, Bells Hill, *c*.1910. In 1894 the baker was Alfred Allen but Horace Newell took over about 1907 and was a grocer as well as a baker. He and his wife Susan, and then his daughter Marjorie, ran the shop until 1965 when it became a greengrocer.

public houses continued until they were demolished in 1967.

The main trades of butcher, baker, grocer, general store and newsagent, post office and boot repairer were all catered for by different shopkeepers over a period of some 130 years. At one time there were two bakers and two grocers. Prior to the First World War Bells Hill had become the hub of the village.

Part of the church land became the ideal site for a village hall. The cost of building it in 1912 was £1,300, most of the money being raised by subscriptions from the gentry. The decision to build

was taken in July 1912 and it was completed by December of the same year. The grand opening was on 22 January 1913 with a smoking concert to which every man over 15 years of age was invited. Despite a snowstorm, the hall was nearly full.

After the First World War a corrugated iron building, 20 by 50 feet, used during the war at Kynoch's factory, was purchased by Canon Barnett at a cost of £250 as a 'club or social centre for village lads aged 14 to 16 years'. This hut was erected near the village hall; later it became the British Legion hut. In 1972 the Reverend Cyril Harris arranged for

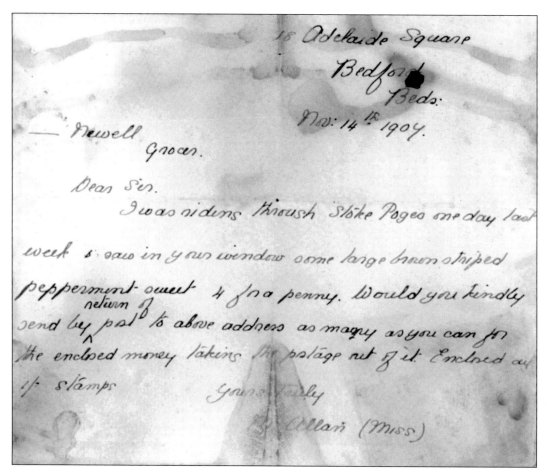

173   Letter received by Newell's the grocer dated 14 November 1907.

174   Miss Newell outside her shop, early 1960s.

an anonymous donor to finance the purchase of the hut and land from the Diocesan Board at a cost of £5,000. Ownership was vested in the Parish Council but it was to be another 25 years before it was used to extend the village hall and provide a new car park.

After the Second World War the population of Stoke Poges almost doubled with the construction of over a thousand new houses. In the early 1950s Eton Rural District Council acknowledged the need for improved shopping facilities but little progress was made until 1960 when a compulsory purchase order was made for the land and buildings on Bells Hill. This order was confirmed in 1962.

175 Bells Hill in 1965 with Miss Newell's shop to the left of the telegraph pole; further up is the *Six Bells*, and set forward is Neville and Bell and Tom Caldecourt's shop.

176 Looking down Bells Hill in the early 1920s. To the right of the *Six Bells* sign is the butcher's shop of James Harman who took over from Daniel Lawrence in 1907 and was succeeded by Roy Neville in 1924.

177 Roy Neville aged 30 outside his shop in 1927 with his assistant Wally Day. Roy Neville became the village butcher in 1924 but in 1929, during the economic crisis of that time, the partnership of Neville and Bell was formed without a written agreement—or a cross word in all the years that followed. Roy Neville served on the Parish Council from 1928-71 and was chairman for 21 years.

178 Roy Neville's shop in the early 1930s, showing (left to right) Roy, his son Peter, his wife Jean, Sam Bell, Steve Cox and Reg Day. The butcher's boy Steve Cox joined the regular army and ended his career as a lieutenant-colonel.

179 Roy Neville outside his shop in 1969 just before it was demolished.

180 The top of Bells Hill just north of its junction with Uxbridge Road (now called Hollybush Hill), *c*.1910. The building with three chimneys (number 1 on the map below) was Squibb's, later Walford's, Hammond's and the Co-op before it was demolished in 1968/9. Next but one is the *Sefton Arms* (number 2 on the map). The cottage with the archway became the post office (number 3 on the map).

In April 1964 a proposed scheme for redevelopment with flats, shops, a new public house, library and public conveniences was presented in the form of a model to a packed public meeting attended by about 200 residents. The public was very critical, especially of the four-storey flats described as 'disgusting skyscraper monstrosities'. In October of the same year the Rural Council put forward a modified scheme for three- rather than four-storey flats to another public meeting attended by 90 people.

The public expressed a preference for nothing higher than two-storey development and this was eventually approved by the County Council and a village green was also incorporated into the scheme. The redevelopment took place between 1967 and 1969 with 26 houses, 16 two-storey flats, 12 shops, including a bank,

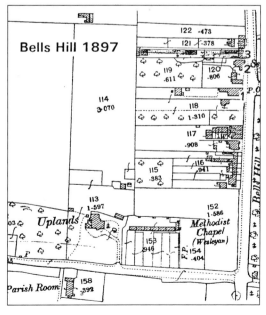

181 Bells Hill, 1897

182 Joseph Squibb took over the general store on Bells Hill in 1887 and the post office transferred to it from the Parochial Rooms in Rogers Lane. This was the grocer's shop built in 1833 by William Ball and run by him and then his son until 1868. Squibb became chairman of the Parish Council from 1896-8. His assistant, a man on the stout side called Aldridge, was emphatic that children said 'please' and 'thank you' when being served.

183 In 1911 Squibb's store changed to Walford's. The post office was relocated to one of the cottages further up the hill.

184 The post office received and sent telegrams by morse code. The mail came from Slough at 7a.m. daily, and then to Gerrards Cross by pony and trap. There were no telephones or electric light, only paraffin and candles. A team of postmen delivered the mail three times each day. In the photograph, reading from left to right, are Mr. Charlie Woodhouse, Mr. Bert Burgess, Mr. Martin, Mr. Piner, Mr. Percy Plumbridge and Mr. George Devening. Under the archway was the rear of the post office where the mail was sorted.

185 The cottage next to the post office was Devening the baker from about 1910 to 1928 when it moved to Wexham Street. The photograph shows the shop at the top of Bells Hill from which deliveries were made as far as Iver Heath, Wexham, Fulmer and Stoke Green. Work started at 6a.m. and the shop remained open until 9p.m. The large baker's oven was used to cook the Sunday joint for those who had no ovens or lacked the necessary fuel.

186 C.T. Caldecourt, the newsagent, took over Devening's shop in 1928. The photograph shows the top of Bells Hill with the shops of Caldecourt and, in what used to be the post office, the insurance business of William Friday. The house on the left in Hollybush Hill became the post office from 1912 to 1969.

187 The *Sefton Arms* in 1902. This was located between the village store and the cottages at the top of Bells Hill. In 1894 William Stevenson, then aged 43 and the landlord of the *Sefton Arms*, was elected to the newly created parish council. In 1904 he became the parish clerk and also assistant overseer or rate collector.

188 The *Sefton Arms* in 1928. Stevenson continued as parish clerk until 1930 when he retired at the age of 79 due to failing eyesight. The car in the photograph belonged to Bert Burgess who was the cycle dealer from 1915 until the 1930s. As he drove up the hill in his car locals would say, 'I think I can ... I think I can'.

189   The *Sefton Arms* in 1961. It was demolished in 1969 to make way for the redevelopment of Bells Hill.

190   Bells Hill shopping precinct in the course of construction in 1969.

191   The extended village hall, now called the Village Centre, 1997.

with flats above, 42 garages, public conveniences and a library.

Retail trading patterns changed in the following years. Shoppers preferred large supermarkets with lower prices and the facility of shopping under one roof. From the 1980s six large supermarkets were built within a few miles of Stoke Poges. Thirty years after Bells Hill Shopping Precinct was completed, half the shops were empty and the bank had closed.

Thirty-Four

The History of Stoke Poges Church

The enduring focal point in the history of Stoke Poges is the church which has been on the site for over 1,000 years but only part of the north wall of the original chancel and a window in that wall remain. During the period of Saxon architecture, with their crude tools and lack of skill, the masons were unable to cut stones to fit closely together and this explains why the window, in particular, is thick and roughly finished. Indeed, it remained blocked for many centuries and it was only through the generosity of Mrs. Allhusen that it was restored in memory of Allied soldiers who died in the Second World War.

It was shortly after William of Normandy had defeated Harold that Hugh de Stoke, who held the manor at that time, his wife, Alicia, and

192 The restored window in the north wall of the chancel.

Aluredus, the first recorded vicar, made over the church and tithes of the parish of Stoke Poges to the Priory of St Mary Overy, Southwark, in 1107. By the beginning of the 12th century there was a revival of monastic life in England and it became quite common for parish churches to be given to monastic foundations. The appropriation of a parish church with its tithes was a great help to a small, often impoverished priory or monastery, but both sides benefited. The parishioners appreciated the fact that, as was the custom, the priory or monastery became responsible for keeping the chancel in good repair although the nave remained the property of the parishioners, who often found it quite a heavy burden. It was at this time, incidentally, that the nave was rebuilt and the surviving pillars again reflect the 'thick' style of Norman architecture.

The masons by the time the south aisle of the nave was built, together with the tower and the extension of the chancel, in the early 13th century, had mastered the art of building in stone. This can be clearly seen in the pointed or lancet windows in the chancel as opposed to the rounded ones of the Norman period—the style of architecture is known as Gothic or Early English. Once a wealthy benefactor like John de Molyns decided to build or restore a part of a church the master mason, although not an architect in the technical sense of the word, would become responsible for the general design of any part built under his supervision. He would design the form and architectural character of the piers, arches, etc., and he would make rough sketches on a board or block of stone for the guidance of craftsmen working under him. These are called bankers marks and some of these can be seen on the pillar in the south aisle.

193 The oak timbered porch, *c.*1900.

194 Interior of porch, 1999.

The growing population, and the fact that everyone from the lord of the manor to the poorest peasant or serf had to attend church, meant that by the end of the 13th century the north aisle in the church of Stoke Poges had to be built. Perhaps it should be mentioned that there were no pews until much later: everyone stood except the weakest who sat on benches by the wall—hence the expression 'the weakest go to the wall'.

In the early part of the 14th century, the porch was added on the south side of the nave; this was intentional as it was the sunnier side of the church. In the Middle Ages, the porch would have played an important part in the life of Stoke Poges. Business transactions were carried out there as a sign of good faith and up to the middle of the 16th century, in the reign of Edward VI, most of the marriage ceremony was performed there. The porch was constructed out of huge oak timbers, and tradition states that those in Stoke Poges were taken from unwanted ships, and they have survived for over 700 years.

Not only does Stoke Poges church reflect the changes in style of architecture but it provides evidence of the many complex rites and observances of the medieval Church centred on the Pope in Rome, some of which were condemned as idolatrous in post-Reformation times whilst others

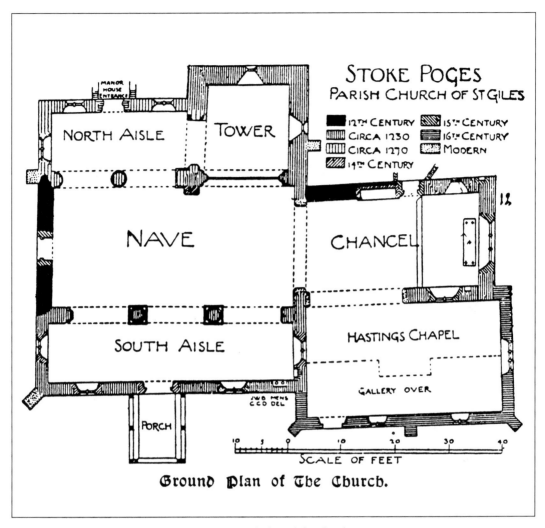

195 Ground plan of the church.

have stood the test of time. Although not the original one, a font has always stood opposite the door, since baptism is the ceremony which gives admittance to the church.

During the Middle Ages it was quite common for a wealthy man in the parish to provide a chantry where priests could say masses for the soul of the founder. The infamous Sir John de Molyns, a 'robber baron', founded one in 1338 in the chapel of St Thomas the Martyr at the east end of the south aisle for the daily celebration

of divine service. Evidence of this chapel can still be seen today: the aumbry where the holy vessels were kept and the double piscina, a great rarity since few churches actually obeyed an order that there should be two basins, one for the ceremonial washing of the priests' hands, the other for the washing of the altar vessels. There are two other piscinas in the church, a beautiful 13th-century Gothic one in the south wall of the chancel, and a third on the outside wall of the chancel where a sacristry once stood.

196 Stoke Poges Church, looking west.

197 The Easter Sepulchre in the north wall of the chancel.

198   The Hastings Chapel.

On the north wall of the chancel is a relative rarity in parish churches, a mid-14th-century tomb recess, used as an Easter Sepulchre, and it is possible that it was the tomb of Sir John de Molyns; he died in disgrace, which may explain why there is no inscription. Easter Sepulchres were always on the north wall, and in pre-Reformation days it was where the Sacrament was placed on Good Friday, then watched continuously until Easter Sunday, when it was taken back to the altar, symbolising the death and resurrection of Christ. After the Reformation this ceremony was regarded as idolatrous and many sepulchres were destroyed—hence the rarity.

Other changes took place at the time of the Reformation which were to affect Stoke Poges church. Since the village was many miles from the Priory of St Mary Overy in Southwark,

parishioners were unlikely to be affected by its dissolution in 1539-40, although the church was once more in the hands of a lay patron. In 1547, in the first parliament of Edward VI, an act was passed which abolished chantries. Instead it became the practice for wealthy people to build almshouses or hospitals with chapels attached where the inmates could pray for their benefactor. This was why the Hastings Chapel was built on the south side of the church, in the angle of the chancel and south aisle, close to the Hospital founded by Lord Hastings in 1558. It was typical of Tudor architecture, being built of brick instead of the chalk and flint used in the rest of the church.

The chapel was incorporated into the rest of the church when the south wall of the chancel was removed at the end of the 18th century and

199 Exterior of Hastings Chapel showing the coat of arms of Lord Hastings of Loughborough.

Devereux in commemorating his son killed in action in 1944. It is now almost exactly as it would have been when it was built; some of the original tiles are still on the floor and the oak door, with its strap hinges, is also original; above the door is Lord Hastings' coat of arms.

Further changes to the inside and outside of the church have been made since the 16th century. From 1702-34, according to the records, there were constant repairs and additions, to the plaster on the ceiling, walls and the galleries (since removed). The door in the chancel, built in the 15th century, opens into the cloisters and in 1907 it connected the newly built vestry with the chancel. The 'ivy mantled tower' originally had a spire; the first one was built in 1701 but this had to be replaced in 1834, and in 1924 that too had to be removed when it was found to be in

in 1946 it was completely restored by William Hartley and Sons under the direction of Martin Travers, thanks to the generosity of Colonel

200   St Giles' Church, 1788.

danger of collapse. At the same time, the bells which were rung from the floor of the tower were moved to a higher storey with access from the outside.

The ground stage of the tower is now occupied by the Penn Pew, which serves as a reminder of the important part that family played in the life of the church from the time when Thomas, son of the famous Quaker William, became lord of the manor and owner of Stoke Park in 1760, until in 1840 the estate passed into other hands. The Penn family vault is close to the font in the nave. Lords of the manor would not have entered by the church door but had their own private entrance through a passage or 'cloister' which led into a small room whose windows according to tradition contain some of the glass brought from the Manor House in 1790.

Once wooden seats had become a permanent feature in the church it became a common practice for particular families to appropriate some pews and pay a rent for their exclusive use—this was called 'pew letting'. The Penn Pew is not the only one associated with a famous name. In the far corner as one enters through the porch is the Thomas Gray Pew. The beautiful box pews, seen in the nave, were the work of Ned Hartley's grandfather at the end of the last century.

Memorials to the dead abound in the church— the earliest is the 13th-century stone slab of a crusader with an inscription in Norman French. The more modern and certainly more aesthetically pleasing ones are: the Pre-Raphaelite painted window in the south wall of the nave, in memory of a little girl of the Howard-Vyse family, the small marble figure, sculptured by Flaxman in memory

THE PENN PEW. STOKE POGES CHURCH.

LL644

201 The Penn Pew.

202 The Bicycle Window, in the west wall.

recorded picture of a hobby horse anywhere in the world. It appears that the glass was part of a larger window design in a house but one can only speculate as its actual history is obscure. The glass shows someone riding a hobby horse while blowing a trumpet.

Stoke Poges church has other memorials which not only tell us the names of wealthy parishioners of the past but also give a very good and accurate representation of the style of armour or costume of the time. During the Middle Ages, instead of tablets or headstones, the wealthy would have brasses, and Sir John de Molyn's grandson, William and his wife, have theirs in the sanctuary close by the altar (1425). Nearby are two other brasses, placed there 150 years later, of the Hampdyns, the same family as the more famous John Hampden. Brasses like these are quite rare since many were destroyed by the iconoclastic hands of the Puritans.

By the late 17th century brasses had gone out of fashion and other ways were found to record the death of members of wealthy families in the parish of Stoke Poges. It became the custom to have the coats of arms of the person who had died

of Nathaniel Marchant, an engraver of gems, and above all the famous Bicycle Window, which serves as a reminder of how many people in Stoke Poges lost loved ones in the Second World War. The window is on the west wall where the west door used to be and incorporated into it is a remarkable piece of stained glass. It is probably the earliest

203 The original Bicycle Window, before part of it was installed in the west window.

painted on to a large lozenge-shaped wooden frame. It was a painting of an 'achievement', i.e. the display of armorial bearings, and it was called a 'hatchment' which is a corruption of the word 'achievement'. On the death of a prominent person, entitled to bear arms in person, it was customary to have the hatchment hung at the front door of their house as a sign of mourning. It then formed part of the funeral procession to the church and, after a period of time, if the vicar agreed, it would be hung in the church.

Stoke Poges church has 19 hatchments, far more than is usual. Not surprisingly, most of them belong to families prominent in the village in the 18th or 19th centuries. The Penn family have the most—six with their Latin motto 'Dum clavum teneam' and their shield 'having a silver field charged with a black fesse on which are 3 silver roundels'.[1] The Gayer family, who were owners of Stoke Park from 1657-1729, have one as does Viscount Cremorne, who married the granddaughter of William Penn, founder of Pennsylvania, and also the Duke of Leeds, whose family is still patron of the living of Stoke Poges. Other hatchments which figure prominently are those of the Howard-Vyse family who lived at Stoke Place. There is nothing written on any of them except the motto but each hatchment has its own story. The man's coat of arms is always impaled with his wife's arms. In the case of Elizabeth Gayer, however, because she never married, there is only a lozenge not a shield, and instead of the helmet or cherub indicating a married lady, there is a lover's knot. John Penn was probably a bachelor since there are no other arms impaled on his shield and the Duke of Leeds must have married a commoner since no arms appear on the left (sinister) side (right or dexter as you look at it)—there is just an ornate leaf pattern.

Like the wife of the Duke of Leeds, other commoners have left a reminder that they too were

204   The hatchment of Elizabeth Gayer.

205   The hatchment of George Godolphin, 8th Duke of Leeds (1802-72). He was of Royal descent and this is indicated in the Royal Crown shown above his coronet.

206 St Giles' Church, *c.*1887.

once members of the village. Amongst all the headstones and tablets in the churchyard are gravemarkers, two wooden posts with a horizontal beam between them, looking rather like a bedhead and on which are inscribed the names of the deceased.

Stoke Poges church has not only been the place of worship for over 1,000 years but it provides us today with so many reminders of those people who have given us the church and the village as we know it today.

Elegy
Written in a Country Churchyard

The curfew tolls the knell of parting day,
The lowing herd winds slowly o'er the lea,
The ploughman homeward plods his weary way,
And leaves the world to darkness and to me.

Now fades the glimmering landscape on the sight,
And all the air a solemn stillness holds,
Save where the beetle wheels his droning flight,
And drowsy tinklings lull the distant folds:

Save that from yonder ivy-mantled tower
The moping owl does to the moon complain
Of such as, wandering near her secret bower,
Molest her ancient solitary reign.

Beneath those rugged elms, that yew-tree's shade,
Where heaves the turf in many a mouldering heap,
Each in his narrow cell for ever laid,
The rude forefathers of the hamlet sleep.

The breezy call of incense-breathing morn,
The swallow twittering from the straw-built shed,
The cock's shrill clarion or the echoing horn,
No more shall rouse them from their lowly bed.

For them no more the blazing hearth shall burn,
Or busy housewife ply her evening care:
No children run to lisp their sire's return,
Or climb his knees the envied kiss to share.

Oft did the harvest to their sickle yield,
Their furrow oft the stubborn glebe has broke;
How jocund did they drive their team afield!
How bowed the woods beneath their sturdy stroke!

Let not Ambition mock their useful toil,
Their homely joys, and destiny obscure;
Nor Grandeur hear with a disdainful smile,
The short and simple annals of the poor.

The boast of heraldry, the pomp of power,
And all that beauty, all that wealth e'er gave,
Awaits alike the inevitable hour.
The paths of glory lead but to the grave.

Nor you, ye Proud, impute to these the fault,
If Memory o'er their tomb no trophies raise,
Where through the long-drawn aisle and fretted vault
The pealing anthem swells the note of praise.

Can storied urn or animated bust
Back to its mansion call the fleeting breath?
Can Honour's voice provoke the silent dust,
Or Flattery soothe the dull cold ear of Death?

Perhaps in this neglected spot is laid
Some heart once pregnant with celestial fire;
Hands that the rod of empire might have swayed,
Or waked to ecstasy the living lyre.

But Knowledge to their eyes her ample page
Rich with the spoils of time did ne'er unroll;
Chill Penury repressed their noble rage,
And froze the genial current of the soul.

Full many a gem of purest ray serene
The dark unfathomed caves of ocean bear:
Full many a flower is born to blush unseen,
And waste its sweetness on the desert air.

Some village-Hampden that with dauntless breast
The little tyrant of his fields withstood,
Some mute inglorious Milton here may rest,
Some Cromwell guiltless of his country's blood.

The applause of listening senates to command,
The threats of pain and ruin to despise,
To scatter plenty o'er a smiling land,
And read their history in a nation's eyes,

Their lot forbade: nor circumscribed alone
Their growing virtues, but their crimes confined;
Forbade to wade through slaughter to a throne,
And shut the gates of mercy on mankind,

The struggling pangs of conscious truth to hide
To quench the blushes of ingenuous shame,
Or heap the shrine of Luxury and Pride
With incense kindled at the Muse's flame.

Far from the madding crowd's ignoble strife
Their sober wishes never learned to stray;
Along the cool sequestered vale of life
They kept the noiseless tenor of their way.

Yet even these bones from insult to protect
Some frail memorial still erected nigh,
With uncouth rhymes and shapeless sculpture decked,
Implores the passing tribute of a sigh.

Their name, their years, spelt by the unlettered muse,
The place of fame and elegy supply:
And many a holy text around she strews,
That teach the rustic moralist to die.

For who to dumb Forgetfulness a prey,
This pleasing anxious being e'er resigned,
Left the warm precincts of the cheerful day,
Nor cast one longing lingering look behind?

On some fond breast the parting soul relies,
Some pious drops the closing eye requires;
Even from the tomb the voice of Nature cries,
Even in our ashes live their wonted fires.

For thee who, mindful of the unhonoured dead,
Dost in these lines their artless tale relate;
If chance, by lonely Contemplation led,
Some kindred spirit shall inquire thy fate,

Haply some hoary-headed swain may say,
'Oft have we seen him at the peep of dawn
Brushing with hasty steps the dews away
To meet the sun upon the upland lawn.

'There at the foot of yonder nodding beech
That wreathes its old fantastic roots so high,
His listless length at noontide would he stretch,
And pore upon the brook that babbles by.

'Hard by yon wood, now smiling as in scorn,
Muttering his wayward fancies he would rove,
Now drooping, woeful wan, like one forlorn,
Or crazed with care, or crossed in hopeless love.

'One morn I missed him on the customed hill,
Along the heath and near his favourite tree;
Another came; nor yet beside the rill,
Nor up the lawn, nor at the wood was he;

'The next with dirges due in sad array
Slow through the church-way path we saw him borne.
Approach and read (for thou canst read) the lay,
Graved on the stone beneath yon aged thorn.'

The Epitaph

Here rests his head upon the lap of earth
A youth to Fortune and to Fame unknown.
Fair Science frowned not on his humble birth,
And Melancholy marked him for her own.

Large was his bounty and his soul sincere,
Heaven did a recompense as largely send:
He gave to Misery all he had, a tear,
He gained from Heaven ('twas all he wished) a friend.

No further seek his merits to disclose,
Or draw his frailties from their dread abode,
(There they alike in trembling hope repose),
The bosom of his Father and his God.

Notes

One   The Origin of the Name 'Stoke Poges', pp.2-3.

1.   Maxwell Fraser, *The History of Slough*, Slough Corporation, 1973, p.5.

Two   The de Molyns Family, pp.4-6.

1.   Natalie Fryde (ed.), *A medieval robber baron Sir John Molyns of Stoke Poges, Buckinghamshire*, Medieval Legal Records, edited in memory of C.A.F. Meekings. HMSO. p.198. Source also of other information in this chapter.
2.   *Ibid.*, p.207.
3.   P.R.O. C139/104/49 19 Henry VI, 28 Oct.1440 Alianor Molyns Proof of Age Writ not reqd.

Three   The Hungerford and Hastings Families, pp.7-9.

1.   'Attainder' was the forfeiture of goods, lands and disinheritance of heirs.
2.   Allen Meredith, 'The Yew at Stoke Poges', *Stoke Poges Parish Newsletter*, No.63, June 1982.

Seven   Thomas Gray and Stoke Poges, pp.18-21.

1.   R.W. Ketton-Cremer, *Thomas Gray—A Biography*, p.99, Cambridge University Press, 1955.

Nine   The Penns, pp.25-29.

1.   Nicholas B. Wainwright, 'The Penn Collection', *The Pennsylvania Magazine of History and Biography*, Volume 87, Number 4, October 1963, p.399.
2.   Grisaille—a painting executed entirely in monochrome in a series of greys.
3.   John Jay Smith, 'The Penn Family', *Lippincott's Magazine*, V (1870), pp.153-4.
4.   Wainwright, 'The Penn Collection', *ibid.*, p.407.

Fifteen   The Enclosure Controversy, pp.42-7.

1.   Lionel Rigby, *The History of Stoke Common—A Poor's Fuel Allotment Charity* (Stoke Poges Parish Council, 1975), for a more detailed account of the enclosure controversy.
2.   The term 'allotment' in the title of the Charity referred to the two allotments of land made in the Enclosure Award to the poor of Stoke Poges. One allotment of just over 32 acres was on the west side of the B416, the other of just over 167 acres was on the east side of the road.

Sixteen   Sidney Godolphin Osborne and the Poor Law Petitions, pp.48-53.

1.   Arnold White (ed.), *Letters to* The Times *Newspaper 1844-88*, (2 vols., 1890), Vol.1, p.xiv.
2.   Godolphin Osborne recalled this incident in a letter to *The Times* in 1868 on the subject of 'Pulpit Cowardice' in which he expressed the opinion that 'the great use of preaching is to uphold right, denounce wrong; to offer hope, or warn against its loss, without respect of persons, according as it is written'. *Letters to* The Times *Newspaper*, Vol.2, pp.17-19.
3.   The account of the meeting in the *Windsor, Slough and Eton Express*, 7 February 1835, recorded that one hundred persons attended and that after Mr. Gilbert's address, which lasted an hour, 'the gentlemen present expressed their entire concurrence in the observations that had fallen from Mr. Gilbert and their readiness to promote the success of the measure'.

Seventeen   Stoke Park 1848–1908, pp.54–5.

1.   Alastair Laing, 'Clubhouse Neo Classicism, Sculpture at Stoke Poges', *Country Life*, 27 January 1983.

2.   'The painting takes its name from the Manchester Arts Treasures Exhibition of 1857, where it was displayed as by Michelangelo and as a discovery made by one of the organisers, the great German scholar Gustav Waagen.' Michael Hirst and Jill Dunkerton, *The Young Michelangelo* (London, National Gallery Publications, 1994), p.10.

3.   D.B. Banwell, *The Red Stags of Rakaia* (New Zealand, 1970).

Twenty-Eight   Fred Spring of Stoke Green, pp.108–11.

1.   The 'Machonocie', named after the manufacturer, was a round sealed tin, 6in. in diameter and 2in. deep, containing a meat and vegetable meal.

Thirty-One   Stoke Park Conservation Area, pp.118–9.

1.   Stoke Poges Parish Council Newsletter, no.66, March 1983: 'The Design of the Proposed Extension at the Manor House' by Martin Ashley of Purcell Miller Tritton and Partners.

Thirty-Two   The Schools in Stoke Poges, pp.120–3.

1.   For a more detailed account of education in Stoke Poges, see John Tarrant, *The Village School—Education in Stoke Poges* (Stoke Poges Parish Council, 1976).

Thirty-Three   The Development of Bells Hill, pp.124–33.

1.   The sixth bell, the treble bell, was bought by public subscription and was brought down by Mears of Whitechapel to the *Plough Inn,* Wexham Street, in 1824, for parishioners to see it. Three sacks of wheat, lent by Mr. James Edgson of Berry Farm, a churchwarden, were thrown down triangular fashion in the corner of the bar and the bell crown downwards was securely fixed between them. The bell was filled to the rim with beer and all-comers were invited to help themselves.

Thirty-Four   The History of Stoke Poges Church, pp.134–44.

1.   See chap. 9, p.29, for a reference to Granville Penn's funeral hatchment in John Jay Smith's account of his stay at Stoke Park, and the colour section for a photograph of the hatchment.

Index

Compiled by Auriol Griffith-Jones

Note: **Bold** page numbers refer to illustrations and information in captions. The colour plates between pages 90 and 91 are shown by their Plate Number, also in **bold**.

Albert of Schleswig-Holstein, H.H. Prince, 56, 57
Albrow, Jeremiah, **93**; on Parish Council, 90, 93, 95
Allen, Alfred, baker, **94**, **125**
Allhusen, Christian, 72
Allhusen, Frederick, in Boer War, 96, 99
Allhusen, Henry, 56, 72, 74, 79, 81, **88**; and Parish
    Council, 72, 74, 89–90, 93, 95
Allhusen, Mrs., 134
Allhusen, Mrs. Henry, 96, **97**
Allhusen family, coat of arms, **II**
almshouse *see* Hastings Almshouse
Antrobus, Mary, 17, 18, **18**, 20, 21, 72
Antrobus, Robert, 18
Antrobus, William, 18
Armstrong, G., schoolmaster, 120-1
Army, occupation of Sefton Park, 69-70
Ashton, Thomas, 20
Austin, Alfred, 74

Baldwin, Mr., postman, **83**, 85
Ball, William, 96, 99, **130**
Ball family, 96, 99
Banister, Wilfred, 85
Barnett, Canon A.T., vicar of Stoke, 108, **108**, 112, 125
Barrett, C.P., **52-3**
Bateman, A., **108**
Bateman, J.L., **108**
Bateman, W.T., **108**
Batten, Mr. and Mrs., 123
Bayer Group, Stoke Court, 79
Baylis House, 100
Bell, Sam, **128**
Bells Hill, 45, 96, **124**, **125**, **127-33**; development,
    124-6, 129, 133; Shopping precinct, 129, 133, **133**
Benevolent Brothers Benefit Society, 80-1, **80**
Blake, Rev. Vernon, 88, **88**, **89**
Boer War, 96, 99
Bold, Rev. Arthur, vicar of Stoke, **37**, 44-5, 48, 63, 120
Bonsey, Mr., 44
Brent, Thomas, innkeeper, 124
brick kiln, Stoke Common, 35, 42
Brickmakers Arms inn, **91**
Brigginshaw, PC, 85
Brougham and Vaux, Henry, Lord, 50, 51
Brown, C., on Parish Council, 93
Brown, Capability (Lancelot), 16, 25
Bryant, Wilberforce, 55, **55**
Buchan, John, 79, 112
Buckingham, Duke of, 50
Buckland, John, blacksmith, 40
Buckland, Mr., shopkeeper, 85, **86**
Bulteel, John George, 67
Bunby, Edward, 86, 87
Bunby, John Thomas, Assistant Overseer, 86-7, 91

Burgess, Bert, **131**, **132**

Caldecourt, C.T., newsagent, **127**, **132**
Cant's Hill, Burnham, 18, 20
Chamberlain, Joseph, 74
charitable bequests: Lady Elizabeth Hatton, 14; Mrs.
    Parker Sedding, 37; for schools, 120; *see also* Hastings
    Almshouse; Poor's Field
charities, 13; Poor's Fuel Allotment, 45, 47; *see also* Stoke
    United Charities
Charities (Lord Hastings Hospital Trust) Order (1980), 13
Charles I, King, 16, **16**
Chesterfield, Lord, **100**
Chesterton, G.K., 112
Childs, F.W., on Parish Council, 93
Church Cottage, **115**, **116**, 117, **117**
Church, Mary, 120
Churchill, Mrs. Winston, 113
Churchill, Winston, 79
Clarke, Edmund, 80
Clifton, Reginald, 105, **105**
Clifton, William, 105, **105**, **106**, 107
Clilverd, John, **82**, 84
Clilverd, Mrs., 99
coaching inns, 18, 100
coal, as fuel, 44, 45
Cobham, Lady, 17, 21, 25
Cobham, Sir Richard Temple, Viscount, 16
Coke, Frances, married Sir John Villiers, 16
Coke, Sir Edward, 14-15, **14**, 16; Monument, 15, **15**,
    25
Coke family, 15
Cole, Robert, agent, 45
Coleman, Edward, 54-5
Colt, Harry Shapland, 56
Cotton, Billy, 70
Cox, Steve, **128**
Crane Davies Limited, **27**, 119
Cremorne, Viscount, hatchment, 143

Dana Corporation, Ohio, Manor House, 118
Daniels, Emily, Assistant Overseer, 91
Darby, Abraham (IV), 72
Day, Reg, **128**
Day, Wally, **128**
de Frece, Sir Walter, 67
de la Mare, Walter, 113
Deare, John, sculptor, 27, **27**
Decies, 5th Lord, 67
Decies, Lord, 4th Lord, 56, 67
deer park, 4, 25, 54-5
Devening, George, postman and baker, **131**
Dibbs, Thomas, 35
Ditton, 38, 100

Ditton Park, 38, 44, **XI**
Dog and Pot inn, 80-1, **81**, 82, 83, 86, **93**
Domesday Book, 2, **3**
Doneraile, Lord, 82
Duckworth, Rev. Henry, 22, 23, 24
Duckworth, Admiral Sir John, 22–3, **I**
Duffield House, **89**, 103
Duncan, Sir William, 69

Easson family, **89**
East Lodge, Sefton Park, **71**
Education Act: (1870), 122; (1944), 123
Edward II, King, 4
Edward III, King, 4
Edward VII, King, 57
Elizabeth I, Queen, 14
Elkins, J., on Parish Council, 93
enclosure, controversy, 42-7
Enclosure Award, 45, **46**, 47, **47**; Bells Hill, 124, **124**; new public roads, 47
Eton College, 8, 20
Eton Poor Law Union, 41, **52-3**
Eton Rural District Council (predecessor of South Bucks D.C.), 59, 65, 126
Ettridge, Arthur, on Parish Council, 90, 93

fair, St Giles's Day, 4
Fellows, Mr. and Mrs., 123
First World War, 104-7, **106**, 108-9, **110**, 111; war memorial, 104, **104**
Fisk, William, on Parish Council, 90, 93
Fitz-Ansculf, William, 2
Five Bells inn, 124
Freeman, William George, 44
Friday, William, **132**
Froude, J.A., 49
fuel: allotment made to poor for turf cutting, 45; turf compared with coal, 44, 45
Fulmer, 47

Galsworthy, John, 79
Garbett, E., **108**
Gardens of Remembrance, 114-17, **114**, **115**, **XVIII**; curfew bell, **115**, 117; Gurkha Memorial, **116**, 117
Gayer, Elizabeth, hatchment, 143, **143**
Gayer, John, 16
Gayer, Sir Robert, 16, 117
Gayer, Robert, 16
George III, King, 54
Gifford, William, Bishop of Winchester, 3
Gilbert, W.J., Poor Law Commissioner, 50, 51
Gilliat, Algernon, 88, 89, **89**, **90**, 103
Glaxo, at Sefton Park, 71
Godolphin, Dr. Henry, **100**
Gosse, Edmund, 112
Gray, Dorothy, 17, 18, **18**, 20, 72
Gray, Thomas, **18**, **19**, 20-1, **20**, 22; 'A Long Story' (poem), 14, 16–17, 21; at West End House, 17, 20, 72; bicentenary celebrations, **21**; 'Elegy in a Country Churchyard', 18, 21, **145-8**; manuscripts sold, 29; Monument, 67, 112, **113**, **119**; sarcophagus, 25
Gray's Meadow, 112-13, **112**
Great Western Railway Company, 56-7, 100, **101**
Grenfell, Emily, m. Sidney Godolphin Osborne, 49
Grey of Falloden, Lord, 112
Groom, Mr., steward at Manor House, 17

Grossmith, Mr., surgeon, **40**
Gurkha Regiment, memorial in Gardens of Remembrance, **116**, 117

Halfway House, Squib's workhouse, **32**, 35
Halsey, Anne, married Sir Richard Temple, 16
Halsey, Edmund, 16
Hampdyn (Hampden) family, 142
Hardy, Thomas, 79
Harman, James, **127**
Harris, Rev. Cyril, **3**, 125-6
Hartley, Ned, **3**, 141
Hartley, William, and Sons, 140
Hassall, Dr. W.O., 15
Hastings, Sir Edward, m. Mary Hungerford, 8, 9
Hastings, Edward, Lord Hastings of Loughborough, 9, **12**
Hastings, Francis, 2nd Earl of Huntingdon, 9, 10
Hastings, George, 1st Earl of Huntingdon, **8**, 9
Hastings, Henry, 3rd Earl of Huntingdon, 14
Hastings, William, Lord, 8-9
Hastings Almshouse, 9, 10, 13; moved to Park Road, **10**, **11**, 13; right to pasture cows, 10, 13
Hatheral, Thomas, lamplighter, 91
Hatton, Sir Christopher, 14
Hatton, Elizabeth, Lady, 14, 15, 16
Hawkins, J., on Parish Council, 93
Hearn, Benjamin, on Parish Council, 88, 90
Hedge, John, 38
Hedgerley, 47
Henley, W., **108**
Henson, Leslie, 113
Highland Division, 51st, at Sefton Park, **67**, 69–70
Holdship, Richard, **80**
Hollybush Hill, 103
Home Farm, Sefton Park, **71**
Hope-Hawkins, Anthony, 112
Horlick's factory, Slough, **101**
housing development, 103
Howard, Field Marshal Sir George, Stoke Place, 25, 60-1, **XII**, **XIII**
Howard-Vyse, Howard Henry, 56, **62**, 63
Howard-Vyse, Major General Sir Richard, **62**, 63, 65
Howard-Vyse, Richard William, MP, 44, 61, **62**, 63
Howard-Vyse family, 141; hatchment, 143
Hughes, Edward, 41
Hundred Court, 3
Hungerford, Mary, 8
Hungerford, Sir Robert, Lord Hungerford and Molyns, 5, 6, 7–8, **7**
Hungerford, Thomas, 8
Huntingdon, Earls of, *see* Hastings
Hutchings, William, **30**, 31

International Hospitals Group, Stoke Park, 119

Jackson, Nick ('Pa') Lane, 55, 56, 57
Judd, W.A., 67, 112

Ketton-Cremer, R.W., 21
Kiln Cottage, **84**
Kingsley, Charles, 49
Kingston, William, Dean of Windsor, 5
Knight, Peter, on Parish Council, 90, 93

Labouchere, Henry, Lord Taunton, 29, 54, **55**
Lack, Thomas and Jane, **82**, 84

L'Amazone (French ship), **23**, 24
Lambe, Patrick, Stoke Place, 60
Land Use Consultants, 119
Landseer, Sir Edwin, 54, 55
Langley, Benjamin, on Parish Council, 93, 95
Langley, James, **82**, 84, 85
Lawrence, Daniel, **127**
Leadbetter, Stiff, 25
Leeds, 8th Duke of, hatchment, 143, **143**
Leicester, Earl of, 15
Lewis, Thomas, master of workhouse, 36
'Lilli Marlene', 69-70
local government, 30, 88; *see also* Parish Council; Vestry
London and Edinburgh Trust, 71
London Landscape Consortium, 118
London and Oxford Railway Bill, petition against, 86-7

McMichael, G.E.C., 71
Major, Arthur, on Parish Council, 88, 90
'Manifesto', Grand National winner, 67
Manningham, Sir Oliver, 6
Manor Court: convened (1771), 32-3; convened (1809), 32, **44**, 45
Manor House, 4, **9**, 16, **59**, **118**; Charles I imprisoned in, 16; John Penn and, 25; owners (1640-1760), 16-17; rebuilt by Francis Hastings, 9; repairs by Dana Corporation, 118; to Eton Rural District Council, 59; *see also* Stoke Park House
Marchant, Nathaniel, 142
Martin, Mr., postman, **131**
Mason, A.E.W., 112
Mason, Sarah, 124
Mauduit, Egidia, married John de Molyns, 4, 5
Mauduit, Sir John, 4
Maugham, Somerset, 79
medieval field system, 42
Miles Laboratories, Stoke Court, 79
Mobbs, Sir Noel, 57-8, 59, **XVII**; and Gardens of Remembrance, 114
Mobbs Memorial Trust, **9**, 54, 59
Molyneux, Lady Louisa, 66, 121
Molyneux, Lady Maria, 66, 121
Molyns, Eleanor (Alianore), married Sir Robert Hungerford, 5-6, 7, 8
Molyns, Richard de, 5
Molyns, Sir John de, 4-5, 134, 136, 139
Molyns, William de, 5; brasses, **6**, 142
Montague, Lord, of Ditton, 38, 44
Montague, William, Earl of Salisbury, 4
Morralls End, 32-3, 47, 120
Morriston-Davies, Dr. William and Mrs. Ellen, **59**

National Trust, 112, 119; Gray's Meadow, 112
Nettleship, William, Master of Hastings Hospital, 44
Neville, Peter, **128**
Neville, Roy, **127**, **128**
Newell, Horace, **125**
Newell, Marjorie, **125**, **126**, **127**
Nickson, Mr., vicar of Stoke, 40
Noris, Thomas, 31, **31**

Oddfellows Arms inn, 81-2, 87
Oppenheimer, Sir Bernard, 67, 112
Osborne, Lord Francis Godolphin, 48; and enclosure controversy, 44-5; estate map, **43**
Osborne, Rev. Lord Sidney Godolphin, 48-9, **48**, 50, 80

Overseers of the Poor, 30, **30**, 31, **34**; and Squib's workhouse, 32-3, 35

Paganall, Fulk, 2
Paganall, Hawse, 2
Parish Council, Stoke Poges, 88-91, 93, 95, 118, 119
parish records, poor relief, 31
Parker, J.J., **108**
Parry, Edward, 56, **92**; churchwarden, **109**, 111; on Parish Council, 89, 91, 93
Paston, John, 4
Penn, Granville, 27, 72
Penn, Granville John, 27-9, 72
Penn, John, **26**, **27**, **37**, **42**; and Coke's Monument, 15; and enclosure of Common, 32, 42-5, 63; and Manor House, 25, 27
Penn, Lady Juliana, 117
Penn, Rev. Thomas, 29
Penn, Thomas, 16; bought Manor House, 25; relocation of almshouse, 10, 13; rights over Common, 32
Penn family, hatchments, 143, **III**, **IV**
Penn-Gray Museum, **26**, 54, **55**, 117, **117**
Perriman, Joseph, poor relief, 36
Phillips, James, 70
Phillips, W.P., workhouse master, **52-3**
Piner, Mr., postman, **131**
Plumbridge, Percy, postman, **131**
Pogeis, Imbert de, 3
Poges, Margaret, married Sir John Mauduit, 4
Poges, Peter, 4
Poges, Robert de, married Amicia de Stoke, 3, 4
Poor Law Act (1601), 30
Poor Law Amendment Act (1834), 49
poor relief, 30-1, **30**, 49-50; mutual help institutions, 51, 80-1; 'Observations and Documents' pamphlet, 50-1; parish workhouse, 36-7, 38-9; services of surgeon, 40-1; Squib's workhouse, 32-3, 35
poorhouse, 31
Poor's Field, 15
Poor's Fuel Allotment Charity, 45, 47
Poor's Row (Southill Cottages), **84**, **85**
population increase, 100, 103, 126
post office, in West End, 82, **82**, 84, **131**, **132**

railway, 57, 86-7, 100, **101**
Red Lion, Stoke Green, **64**
Repton, Humphry, 25, **V**; and Stoke Park, 25, **57**, 117, 118
Richmond, Nathaniel, 25
Rigby, Lionel, **3**
roads: diversions, **61**, 63, 80, 81; new public, 47
Robarts, Mr., surgeon, 40-1, 51
Rocque, John, map, **17**
Rogers, Mrs. Anna, 17, 18, 20, 22, 72
Rogers, Jonathan, 18, 20, 72
Rogers Lane: 35, 42, 45, **83**; school, 120-1

St Andrew's church, 105
St Giles's church, **28**, **137**, **138**, **140**, **144**, **XIX**; bellringers, **108**, **109**, 111; bells, 124, 141, 150n; Bicycle Window, 142, **142**; chantry chapel, 137; churchyard, **8**, 112, 144; Easter Sepulchre, **138**, 139; Hastings Chapel, 9, 139-40, **139**, **140**; hatchments, 142-3, **143**, **III**, **IV**, **XIII**; memorials, 141-4; North aisle, 136; Penn Pew, 141, **141**; piscinas, 137; porch, **135**, 136, **136**; refounded (1331), 4; Saxon window, 134, **134**; spire, 140–1; Thomas Gray pew, **20**, 141;

yew in churchyard, 9
St Giles's Day fair, 4
St Mary Overy, Priory of, Southwark, 3, 134, 139
Salisbury, Alice, Countess of, 6
Salter, Captain Elliott, 23-4
Salter, Mary, 120
Salter family, 20, 72
Santa Margaretta, HMS, 23-4, **23**
Say, Elizabeth, Lady, 6
Schaub, Lady, 17, 21
School Lane, 45, 123
schools, 120-3, **120**, **121**; Centenary (1976), **122**, 123, **123**; charity, 45; dame schools, 121; First School, **122**, 123; Middle School, 123; Mrs. Parker Sedding's bequest for, 37; National School, 121-2; Rogers Lane, 120-1; in School Lane, 54, **120**, 123; Stoke House, 89
Sedding, Mrs. Parker, 36-7, **37**, 120
Sefton, 2nd Earl of, 66
Sefton Arms inn, 124, **129**, **132**, **133**
Sefton Park, 66-71, **66**, **XV**; sale of, **68**, **69**, 70-1, **70**, **71**, 103; War Office occupation of, 69-70
Settlement and Removal Act (1662), 30
Shaw, Colonel A.G., **59**
Simmons, Charles, **94**, **95**; on Parish Council, 90, **90**, 93
Sired the Saxon, 2
Six Bells inn, 124, **127**
Skales, Thomas, Lord, 6
Slough, 18, 59; part of Stoke Poges transferred to, 100; workhouse (Upton Hospital), 53
Slough Trading Estate, 57, 59, 100
Smirke, Robert, 27
Smith, F.E., 79
Smith, John Jay, 28-9
Somerie, John de, 2
South Bucks District Council (successor to Eton R.D.C.), 59, 65, 126
South Lodge, Sefton Park, **70**
Speed, Henrietta, 17, 21
Spring, Fred, 108-9, **108**, **110**, 111
Squib, James, spinning and weaving workhouse, 31, 32-3, 35
Squibb, Francis, clerk to Parish Council, 91, 93, 95
Squibb, Joseph: general store, 84, **94**, **129**, **130**; on Parish Council, 90, 93, 95
Stevenson, William, Parish clerk, 90, 91, 93, 95, **132**
Stoke, Amicia de, married Robert Poges, 3, 4, 134
Stoke, Hugh de, 3, 134
Stoke, Richard de, 3
Stoke, Thomas de, 3
Stoke: manor of, 2-3; place name, 2, 3; *see also* Stoke Poges
Stoke Common, **47**, **101**; commoners' rights, 42, 44; enclosure controversy, 42–7, **45**; piece enclosed for Squib's workhouse, 32; Site of Special Scientific Interest (1972), 47; *see also* Bells Hill
Stoke Court (formerly West End House), 17, 20, 23, 29, 72-9, **72**, **76**, 80; as Country Club, **79**; sale (1927), **73**, **75**, **77–8**, 79, 103
Stoke Farm *see* Sefton Park
Stoke Green, **63**, **110**; conservation area, 60, **64**
Stoke House, school, 89, **92**
Stoke Hundred, 3
Stoke Park: Conservation Area, 118-9, **119**; deer park, 4, 25, 54-5; gardens, 25, 27, **V**, **VI–X**; Golf Club, 55, 56-7, 59, 118-9; Grade One listing, 119;

Repton's Bridge, 25, **57**, 117, 118; right to pasture cows in, 10, 13; Sir Edward Coke's Monument, 15; *see also* Gardens of Remembrance
Stoke Park House, 28-9, **56**, **57**, 59, 103, **VI-X**; built by John Penn, 25, 27; library, 27, 28, 29; *see also* Manor House; Stoke Poges Golf Club
Stoke Place, 60, **60**, **62**, 63, 65, **XIV**
Stoke Poges: extent of parish, 18, 100, **102**, 103; origin of name, 3
Stoke Poges Golf Club, 55, 56-7, **58**, 59, **59**, 118-9
Stoke Poges Land Company Limited, 55
Stoke Road, **91**
Stoke in Slough, 100
Stoke United Charities, 15, 37
Stowe Park, 16
Strange, Lt L.A., 105, 107

Tarrant, F., **108**
Temple, Sir Richard, Viscount Cobham, 16
Templeman, T., on Parish Council, 93, 95
Thorwaldsen, Bertell, sculptor, 54, **55**
Tilley, Vesta, 67, **67**, 69, **XVI**
tithes, 42
Todd, Margaret, 120
Towton, Battle of, 7
tradesmen, advertisements in Parish Magazine, **94**, **95**
transport, 31, 56-7; motor omnibuses, 56-7, **58**
Travers, Martin, 140
turbary (turf cutting), rights of, 42, 44
Turner, Tom, 40
Tyack, Mrs., housekeeper at Manor House, 17

Uplands house, **33**, 35

Vestry: and Mr. Robarts, 40; and parish workhouse, 36-7, **37**; poor relief, 30-1; and Squib's workhouse, 32-3
vicarage: by Wyatt, **49**; old, 25
Village Hall, 45, 47, 125-6, **125**, **133**
Villiers, Sir John, Viscount Purbeck, 16
Vyse, General Richard, married Anne Howard, 61
Vyse, Miss, 121

Wakefield, C.T., on Parish Council, 93
Walpole, Horace, 20, 21
Walter, tenant of Stoke at Domesday, 2
Ward, Frederick, in Boer War, 96, 99
Ward, Louisa (daughter), 99
Ward, Mrs. Louisa, 96, **98**
Ward, Wilfred, **98**, 99
Ware, John, 41
Wars of the Roses, 7-9
West End, 80–5, **83**, 84, 86-7, **86**
West End House, 17, 20, 23; *see also* Stoke Court
Wexham, Poor's Field, 15
White, Edward, garden designer, 114
Wilson, William, 80
'Winterclyde', **78**, 81-2, **87**
Woodhouse, Charlie, postman, **131**
workhouse: parish, 35, 36-7, 50-1; rules of, 38-9, **38**; Squib's, 32-3, **32**, **33**, 35; Union, 41, 49-53, **52-3**
Wyatt, James: Coke's Monument, 15, 25; Gray's Monument 25, 112, **145**; Stoke Park House, 25; Stoke Park Lodges, **56**; vicarage, **50**
Wyot, William, 5

Yandell, H.H., on Parish Council, 93